feathering THE nest

feathering THE nest

Tracy Hutson's Earth-Friendly Guide to
Decorating Your Baby's Room

TRACY HUTSON

WITH L.G. MANSFIELD

PHOTOGRAPHS BY LAURIE FRANKEL

STEWART, TABORI & CHANG, NEW YORK

Published in 2009 by Stewart, Tabori & Chang
An imprint of Harry N. Abrams, Inc.

Library of Congress Cataloging-in-Publication Data
Hutson, Tracy.
  Feathering the nest : tracy hutson's earth-friendly guide to decorating your baby's room / Tracy Hutson ; with L.G. Mansfield.
     p. cm.
  ISBN 978-1-58479-745-6
  1. Nurseries. 2. Interior decoration. I. Mansfield, L. G. II. Title.
  NK2117.N87H88 2009
  747.7'70832—dc22
                        2008029758

Editor: Dervla Kelly
Designer: Alissa Faden
Production Manager: Tina Cameron

The text of this book was composed in Filosofia and Gotham.

Printed and bound in China
10 9 8 7 6 5 4 3 2 1

HNA
harry n. abrams, inc.
a subsidiary of La Martinière Groupe

115 West 18th Street
New York, NY 10011
www.hnabooks.com

TO BARRY, OLIVER, AND FELIX . . . my sweet angels. Thank you for
making me a mommy. You are my inspiration.

IN MEMORY OF JENESSA NICOLE (BOEY) BYERS, my little warrior,
born May 20, 1999, passed away December 28, 2007.
How much you accomplished in your short lifetime!

*"Birds are so much wiser than we! A robin builds a nest
for robins. A seagull builds a nest for seagulls. They
don't copy each other — or build themselves nests as
described in* The Birds' Decorating Magazine.*"*

—Dorothy Draper, American interior decorator

contents

18

52

80

108

136

CHAPTER 3
traditional

CHAPTER 4
international

CHAPTER 5
trace's tips

INTRODUCTION

Perfection. No other word captures the true essence of how we feel about every aspect of our children's lives. We want the perfect delivery. Ten perfectly formed little fingers and toes. A perfect baby disposition. And, of course, the perfect nursery to welcome our little bundle of joy.

While true perfection may be elusive, every baby—and everything about that baby—is a flawless masterpiece in a parent's eyes. If at times we seem a little obsessive about it, it's completely justified. Bringing a new life into the world is an incredible experience and blessing, and wanting to pave the way with all things wonderful is a natural response.

When I found out that we were expecting our first baby, I felt an amazing rush of excitement, exhilaration, and anticipation. I constantly mused about what life with this little one would be like, and my brain fired nonstop with ideas for the nursery. Even though I've designed many babies' and children's rooms over the years for close friends, clients, and the lovely families on *Extreme Makeover: Home Edition*, this was different, special. This was for our baby, for our family, in our home.

When our second baby arrived, I was faced with a new design challenge. Having decided that newborn Felix and two-year-old Oliver would share a room, I then had to determine ways to meet the needs of both boys in the same space. I wanted the nursery to be stimulating, yet comforting. Intriguing, but not dizzyingly busy. I wanted it to be a place that would maximize safety for an infant and shield an adventurous toddler from harm. Finally, I wanted to make sure that it was all put together with a healthy dose of environmental responsibility. If you're getting the impression that I wanted it all, you're absolutely right!

But as a mother, I knew that my quest for the ideal nursery made perfect sense. After all, this would be a nest for Oliver and Felix—the very first place they would dwell upon leaving the nurturing cradle of my body. It was important to carefully consider every aspect of their room's design so it would be a joyous, wondrous, and protective haven.

As we pursue the dream of a perfect-in-every-way life for our children, the nursery is the logical place to start. But designing the right space can be overwhelming, especially if you're doing it for the first time. (And let's face it—raging hormones don't help.) So I'll be here to help guide you through the process, sharing my knowledge and experience to make feathering your baby's nest a fun and easy undertaking.

In *Feathering the Nest*, you'll find ideas that are beautiful and inspirational, as well as solutions that suit a variety of

"When I count my blessings, I count you twice." —Irish proverb

budgets and tastes. From vintage to international, from traditional to contemporary, you'll see examples of four different styles that translate beautifully to a baby's room.

In each section, I'll focus on the eight major components that make up the design of a nursery. You'll learn how a *color palette* can define a room. How *furniture* and *lighting* can make a dramatic statement. How *bedding* and *window treatments* can punctuate your chosen design. How *flooring* and *storage* can help tie a look together. I'll share secrets about *special touches* that can take your nursery from ordinary to spectacularly extraordinary. And I promise you won't find anything cutesy or gimmicky anywhere in the mix.

I'll walk you through the process step by step, ultimately building to a room that captures the true essence of each design style. I'll even include variations for a boy, girl, and a let's-keep-it-a-surprise baby, so you can make the subtle changes needed to tailor the look for your child.

To enable you to lend a truly personal touch to your baby's room, I've added a do-it-yourself project at the end of each section. Okay—so maybe you're not the Martha Stewart of babydom. Maybe you shudder at the mere thought of walking into a crafts shop. But the fact remains that a little bit of ingenuity (mine) and a smattering of creativity (yours) can go a long way toward adding that special something to the nursery. And think about how pleased and proud you'll feel to bring a lamp or piece of furniture back to life—just for your baby.

As a special bonus, I'll take you into Oliver and Felix's room to show you the nest I've created for my own children. I'll talk a little bit about decorating for multiples, organizing baby's closet and dresser drawers, making the most of the space you have in a small nursery, and giving new life to baby furniture. All the information will give you the confidence to navigate the world of design and create a room that both caters to your little one's every need and reflects your personal style. And yes, everyone has one!

Beyond Design

Of course, the nursery's beauty and functionality are a top priority, but it is equally important to look at the bigger picture. Just as I examined all aspects of the process when planning my sons' nursery, you need to do the same. Are you thinking green? Have you paid close attention to safety? What about stimulating baby's brain?

Because these three components are such an integral part of the design process, I've included them as color-coded sidebars throughout the book. Each one focuses on complementing the overall look of the room with a tip that is practical and/or responsible.

To round out my offerings, I've ended the book with a list of vendors who specialize in everything for baby: from bedding to clothing, from furniture to flooring, from diapers to toys. All of them have an environmental, safety, and/or organic slant, so you can feel good about using their products. And just for the record, they're quite fabulous folks, to boot.

So keep that commitment to perfection and get ready for a delightful experience. You can do it, with the help of *Feathering the Nest* and the many resources available to support your efforts. And no matter what path you take—or no matter where the design takes you—the end result will be a charming nursery that's perfect for your baby in every way.

ENVIRONMENTAL RESPECT

It would be a great disservice to our children and all future generations if we did not do everything in our power to instill an earth-conscious ethic—and it can all begin in the nursery. Besides setting an example of environmental stewardship, such action also helps protect baby's developing immune, hormonal, and nervous systems, which are extremely sensitive to environmental pollutants.

Small changes can make a big difference. That's why it's such a smart idea to decorate with items you already have on hand, gently used hand-me-downs, or vintage and thrift store finds. I'll help you determine ways to give them new life while preserving the life of the planet in the process.

Just a quick note here—I'm more a concerned mom than I am a rabble-rouser. My intent when presenting environmental information is to be informative, not incendiary. My research has shown that there are many conflicting reports regarding the safety of some products, and I certainly don't claim to be an expert for either side. What I do claim is that the health and well-being of our babies and Mother Earth are of primary importance, so my goal is to share with you the things I've learned along the way. Your job, as a parent, is to do your own evaluation—gather more information, if necessary—and make an informed decision.

One thing I've come to understand is that many extenuating circumstances affect a product's impact on the environment. For example, if an item of furniture manufactured outside the United States is shipped by sea, it may have less of a negative impact on air quality than if it were made domestically and transported by truck. So again, find out as much as you can about a product's history and use that knowledge to become a more educated consumer.

SAFETY

Nothing is more important than safety in baby's world. That's why this book is filled with smart ways to help ensure that the nursery is free of anything that might cause harm. Some of the ideas are based on simple common sense and others incorporate a bit more inventiveness, but all are designed with the safety of your little one in mind.

BRAIN STIMULATION

From infancy to eighteen months of age, babies need the stimulation that comes from movement, touch, and color. While the day-to-day experiences you provide for your child fulfill the need for the first two, the ways in which you decorate the nursery can provide the color and visual awareness that are so vital to baby's overall development.

REFLECTIONS ON NESTING AND NURTURING

Life as a parent is messy—wonderfully, fantastically, heart-warmingly messy. We start out with plans for utter perfection, then soon realize it's been three days since we've had a proper shower, and we just don't care one bit.

With a new baby, everything takes on enhanced light and color. Little things grab you by the heartstrings and take your breath away. Your baby's sweet smile. A yawn. The giggle that builds right before your eyes and explodes in a grin that seems larger than he is. The little grunts, gurgles, and suckling motions he makes when he's asleep. The gentle flicker of his eyelids while he dozes that makes you wonder what movie is playing in his little head. The way his cheek feels against yours. The pouty lips and chubby toes. The incredibly tiny size of his first diapers—can a bottom really be that small? If only you could bottle it all up and keep it forever!

If you're currently waiting for your baby's arrival, my advice is to enjoy this time. It's so easy to get caught up in focusing on the big day, but trust me, it will come soon enough. For now, relish the stage you're in. It's the last time—for a long time—that you don't have to be concerned with feeding, changing, or putting your baby to sleep. He has all of that handled on his own right now, so your most important job is to take care of you.

If you're an adoptive parent, the same advice applies. As you wait for your baby to be born or the paperwork to be finalized, relish this pre-mom time. Relax, have fun, and find comfort in the fact that being a mom is the most natural thing in the world.

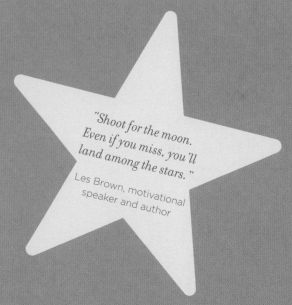

"Shoot for the moon. Even if you miss, you'll land among the stars."
Les Brown, motivational speaker and author

LOTS OF STUFF,
NOT LOTS OF NEEDS

Throughout the nesting period, your autopilot will direct you to the baby stores. You might as well give in, because I don't think there's any way to resist the temptation. Even when your nursery is already brimming with everything you could possibly imagine, the anticipation of the new arrival overcomes any logic. If you just can't stay away, maybe you should go only when you've left your wallet and credit cards at home. Because the fact is you're going to get lots of gifts when your baby arrives. Add those to the stash you've already accumulated, and that's one heck of a lot of stuff! And, in truth, you'll be amazed by how little your baby actually needs in the first few months.

We have really grown into—dare I say it?—an indulged society. We have so many conveniences at our fingertips, and strides in technology have placed even more wondrous things within our reach. Ask your mom what she had to rely on when she brought you home from the hospital. Odds are, it's not a fraction of what we have today.

It's a different world than the one we knew as children. I grew up in the midst of Jumboville—with block-long SUVs, super-sized fast food, and the notion of bigger and better everything. I don't think I ever heard words like "sustainable" or "organic" or "environmental" anything. "Recycling" meant nothing more than giving your outgrown clothes to your little cousin. And "global warming"—jeez!—who knew that was even in the realm of possibility?

Perhaps it's time to take a step back and revisit the concept of less is more. It certainly rings true with babies, and if the basics were good enough for us as little ones, they should be good enough for our own children. So let's take advantage of the opportunity to do our part—however small it may be—to make a difference through the eyes of our children. Let's use our imaginations to find ways to tread a bit more lightly in this world. Imagination is a quality we want to encourage in our little ones, and we might as well set a good example. This planet is their home, and it is our job to safeguard it for them so they will treat it with the same respect for the sake of their own children and generations to follow.

I am now at the stage with Oliver where I'm trying to influence him to make concerned decisions—sharing with his peers and working on being empathetic. If he has a toy that he's outgrown or lost interest in, we make a point of giving it to a child who will enjoy it. I want him to learn at an early age not to take anything for granted and to develop a healthy respect for others and for the earth.

GATHERING WISDOM

Good advice is the best way to avoid mishaps and frustration. When I was pregnant with Oliver, a good friend told me to take a fourth trimester to give myself time to get over the crazy hormones, break out of the fog, and allow time for the baby and me to adjust.

At the time it didn't mean too much to me, but when I embarked upon those first three months of being a new mommy, I realized they were words to live by. It made perfect sense to devote everything—my time, my attention, my sleep-deprived body—to this little wonder whose very existence depended on me.

I look back on those days with such awe and emotion. The time goes by so quickly, and I hope you'll soak it all up and savor every moment. Enjoy the swelling of your heart when your little one gazes into your eyes with unbridled love. The tenderness of tiny hands reaching out to clutch your fingers. The language of your baby's different cries that you can interpret better than anyone else.

Bestow as many kisses as you can, because "cool" toddlers often don't let mommies show affection—at least not in places where they might be spotted by their equally cool preschool buddies. I know that the day will come when my boys think they don't need me. And, of course, I know they'll grow to depend on me less and less. But what our children don't know—and what might remain the mommy

secret—is that they'll be our babies forever. They can be thirty and married with children of their own, but their independence will never change how we feel about them. And that's one of the true glories of motherhood.

Although this is a book about design, I felt it was important to pass along these musings to you. As mothers, we share the bond of being charter members of the baby club, united by all the things we suddenly have in common when we become parents. We can strike up conversations with complete strangers as our paths cross another pregnant belly in the supermarket. "Is this your first?" "What kind of prenatal vitamins are you taking?" "Are you planning a natural birth?" Once we give birth, the commonalities take on a slightly different form. We can enter into conversations about poo-poo in the ob-gyn's office with a woman we've never seen before, and it feels completely natural.

As club members, sharing and comparing become a big part of our lives. The beauty of it all is that we can learn so much from each other, and that's what I'm hoping to accomplish with this book. My wish is to be your guide, your helpmate, and your new friend, to toss ideas your way that encourage and inspire you to take on the project of designing your baby's nursery with confidence and a sense of fun. Just think of it as one more step in the marvelous adventure of parenthood!

inspiration—getting started

The interior-design process is like any other work of art: it begins with a single, simple stroke, and gradually evolves into the finished product. Sometimes, you have a plan. Other times, you simply follow where the first step leads you. Of course, it helps to have at least a general direction in mind, but beyond that, allow yourself a whole lot of freedom.

Inspiration for your baby's room can come from a variety of sources. It might be a blanket that belonged to your grandmother, a framed drawing that your little brother made in preschool, a lamp from a flea market. It might be a beautiful new crib, an antique rocking chair, a just-right-for-painting dresser passed down from a friend. It might be something as simple as a paint chip in a color you love, an area rug that reminds you of your own childhood, a delicate string of paper cranes. Just about any single piece can get you started, directing you to the ultimate mood of the room. Think of the nursery as a blank canvas, awaiting the personality that will emerge over time.

I was seven months pregnant with my son Oliver when we moved into our new home, and I spent countless hours in the empty room that was soon to be his. I noticed how the blank, white walls changed color at different times of day, shifting from bright and cool to soft and warm as the sun moved across the sky.

Taking the time to see how natural light plays within your baby's space can help lead you in the right direction toward color depth and window treatment. And you just might find that inspiration strikes as you sit in the empty space, observing the magic of Mother Nature's paintbrush before you pick up one of your own.

As ideas begin to stir, take a look around your home before you rush out to buy baby furniture. Is there an old chair in the living room that could be re-covered for the nursery? Is there an abandoned chest of drawers in the garage that might come to life with a coat of paint? Is there a bookshelf in the study that would make excellent storage for toys? Besides providing an inexpensive start to your decorating project, this scavenger hunt is a great way to recycle and add a unique personal touch to baby's room. Who knows, a reappropriated find just might turn out to be a family heirloom as the years go by.

Most important, let go of any preconceived notions that a baby's room must have a theme. If you try to adhere too strictly to a particular look, you could end up backing yourself into a design corner, unable to find a place for that lovely quilt Aunt Sally made because it doesn't fit in with your princess or race-car-driver motif. Instead, let your imagination run free and go where your heart takes you. In my experience, living spaces often begin to take

"Décor must have sentimental value. A house must tell a story."

—Mark Hampton, American interior decorator

shape when you listen to your emotional responses to a particular item. As Lauren Bacall has so brilliantly stated, "Imagination is the highest kite one can fly."

I've always believed that a room feels more comfortable when you acquire its contents over time. You'll find that the outcome is more natural than furnishing it all at once. Keep in mind, too, that you'll be getting lots of baby gifts, and some might add a wonderfully imaginative spin to the nursery. In spite of your most carefully calculated decorating plans, the end result could turn out to be an eclectic mix that you'd never even dreamed of—and positively love.

Don't lose sight of the fact that there are no new design ideas, just new interpretations. What's more, don't feel that there is a "right way" to decorate your baby's room. What makes it right is the use of environmentally responsible furniture and accessories, a focus on safety, and a little brain stimulation thrown in for good measure. After all, we want to protect this planet for future generations. We want to keep our babies free from danger. And we want their developing brains to be as intrigued and inspired as possible.

While all of these things can be enhanced by design elements in the nursery, it is we, as parents, who have the greatest impact. The ways in which we interact with our little ones will make more of a difference than a bright red stripe on the wall or a toy designed to fire baby's synapses.

With that in mind, relax and have fun with your design project. Give rein to your creativity. Be playful. Take chances. Love that royal-purple paint you saw in a model home? Buy a quart and experiment. Enchanted by the giant stuffed panda you spotted in the museum gift shop? Decorate around it. As long as your heart is in the process, you're bound to produce a fabulous result.

Let this book serve as a general guide to inspire your design ideas. You might see a wall color in the contemporary section that you find irresistible, so go ahead and use it in your vintage nursery. Or maybe you've fallen in love with a pair of table lamps in the traditional section that you simply must have in your baby's international nursery. That's absolutely fine. The décor police will not knock on your door and demand that you change a thing.

Feel free to mix and match. All of the styles I present are interchangeable, so you can create your own brand of vintage traditional, contemporary international, and so on. Don't feel bound by rules, because they truly don't exist. When you're feathering your baby's nest, the only real must-do is to feel good about whatever you create.

CHAPTER 1

vintage

"Even the simplest
wicker basket can become
priceless when it is loved
and cared for through the
generations of a family."

Sister Parish, American
interior decorator

Vintage design is a charming blend of rusticity and elegance. Don't confuse it with retro (à la bubble chairs and lava lamps), which is better defined as period design. Vintage is all about flea-market finds and antique-shop discoveries, old family heirlooms and attic treasures. It has a carefree feel, with a hint of the romantic countryside, which makes the style very warm and welcoming. It also has a sense of timelessness that seems to heighten the feeling of unparalleled comfort. If you opt for a vintage nursery, don't feel limited by your choices.

It's perfectly fine to add a contemporary element here and there. To help ensure that the two styles work well together, unite them with a common feature. For example, if you're using striped vintage fabric on the windows, feel free to add a contemporary painting with bold, graphic lines that repeat the striped pattern in some way. If you've found a 1940s flowered wallpaper covered with cabbage roses, team it with modern throw pillows in the same floral color palette.

Mother Nature would likely put vintage design at the top of her list, since it's an easy, eco-friendly way to recycle just about every element of the nursery—from furniture to fabrics, from mirrors to accessories.

color palettes

The walls of a vintage room come to life in soft, muted hues of blue, green, pink, and lavender—just like you might find in a watercolor painting or outside your window on a bright summer day. Cream and off-white also work well, and can be used as the base color on either the walls or in furniture.

For a girl's room, try a palette that blends petal pink and seafoam green or pale lilac and silvery moss. For a boy, play with varying shades of faded blue or green, adding touches of butter yellow. To keep your palette gender-neutral, paint the walls a light peach with accents the color of chocolate milk. And it's perfectly okay to decorate with a mix of blues and pinks regardless of whether your child is a boy or girl.

Fabrics in a vintage nursery have a sun-bleached look in shades that seem to come straight from the garden, with patterns that include stripes, polka dots, and paisleys. Use them for upholstered pieces, window coverings, and/or pillows.

Think about balance when deciding on your color palette. If the furniture in the nursery is dark, paint the walls a lighter color. If the woods are light, go with a darker color on the walls and add brightness with a sky-blue ceiling.

LET THE SUN SHINE IN

Get the most out of natural daylight by painting baby's walls a lighter color to reflect more light.

mix & match

Vintage lends itself perfectly to incorporating a variety of patterns. To keep things from getting too busy, keep the mix in the same color palette. For example, if you're working with sage, yellow, and terra cotta, opt for those shades in stripes for the bedding, a small floral for the window covering, and a large floral for the seat cushion of a rocking chair.

Many beautiful textiles are available online, and can provide the inspiration for your nursery's design. Alternatively, a lovely vintage-reproduction wallpaper can serve as your starting point.

petal pink

sky blue

light peach

seafoam green

butter yellow

chocolate milk

pale lilac

silvery moss

vanilla

Furniture

Some of the best furniture for your vintage-style nursery can be found at flea markets. They're a great source for wicker, iron, and spindle cribs, as well as distressed pieces, whitewashed wood, and beadboard. The key to the authenticity and value of a piece is quality wood, so be sure to examine everything closely before you buy. Even if it's covered with a coat of ghastly paint, it's fairly easy to tell what lies beneath. Also look for lines that you find pleasing. The worth of a flea-market find is more about what you like than how old or expensive it is.

When you're wandering through the goodies and the junk, think outside the box. Woods and wicker go together beautifully, so don't lock into one design solution. An old vanity can be transformed into an ideal changing table, especially

CRIB SAFETY

- Be sure the crib mattress fits properly and snugly so baby's head or limbs can't get wedged between the mattress and the sides of the crib.

- Measure the slats. They should be no more than two and three-eighths inches apart so baby doesn't get her head stuck.

- Choose a crib with corner posts that are free of any embellishments that might snag clothing or blankets. Corner posts should not be more than one-sixteenth of an inch high.

- Avoid headboards and footboards with cutouts large enough for baby's head to get trapped.

- Do not place soft bedding, pillows, toys, or stuffed animals in the crib.

- Use sleepers instead of blankets to keep baby warm.

- Follow the product guidelines for crib toys and discontinue use at the recommended age. If toys attach to crib railings, hang them on the wall side of the crib.

- Position the crib away from windows, lamps, blinds and drapes with cords, electrical cords, and furniture that's easy to climb on.

- Do not place the crib near a radiator or heat vent, or under a heating or air-conditioning vent, to prevent baby from getting too hot, too cold, or breathing in dust from the vent.

- If you live in a cold climate, avoid placing the crib against an outside wall during the winter months.

- Lock the drop side of the crib whenever you are not in the room to prevent baby from knocking it and falling out.

- As soon as your infant can push up on his hands and knees, remove any mobiles or toys that hang across the crib.

- Use crib bumpers that are firm, not soft, and secure them tightly. Once your baby can pull herself up—usually at about six months—remove them.

- Regularly check all hardware (nuts, bolts, screws) to make sure they're tight and secure.

- If you buy a vintage or older model crib, make sure it meets current safety standards. For timely updates on cribs that have been recalled, visit the U.S. Consumer Product Safety Commission's Web site at www.cpsc.gov.

Information courtesy of the Home Safety Council, homesafetycouncil.org

HIDDEN HAZARDS
OF ADULT BEDS

The U.S. Consumer Product Safety Commission has alerted parents and caregivers to the hidden hazards associated with placing infants on adult beds. Entrapments, falls, bedding, and the position of the baby on the bed can all be contributing factors. Pushing the bed against the wall or placing pillows along the sides of the bed does not provide sleep safety for babies. Suffocation can result from hidden hazards, including:

- Entrapment between the bed and wall or between the bed and another object

- Entrapment involving the bed frame, headboard, or footboard

- Falls onto piles of clothing, plastic bags, or other soft materials

- Suffocation in soft bedding, such as pillows, thick quilts, and comforters

- To maximize your baby's safety, never put him to sleep on an adult bed under any circumstances. With so many portable carriers available these days, there's absolutely no reason to take the risk.

if you happen across one with scalloped molding or painted details. Look for a chair, daybed, or small upholstered sofa that you can use for snoozing and lounging with baby. An armoire with a mirrored front is great for storing items that are useful but have little visual appeal. Nesting tables serve multiple purposes, but take up very little space because they stack beneath one another.

The more often you visit flea markets, the more skilled you'll become at spotting true treasures. In some cases, the seller doesn't realize the value of a particular piece, but you just might. And as any dedicated shopper will tell you, there's nothing quite as satisfying as finding a great deal on something you love.

If you're not the flea market type, you can create the same mood with reproductions. Unlike genuine antiques, reproductions are free of lead paint, small parts, and sharp edges.

While we're on the subject, this would be a good time to point out how you can remedy some of the problems that are inherent in authentic antique furniture. Painted pieces can be tested for lead using kits available commercially. If the item tests positive, get a professional involved to strip and repaint it. If the edges of furniture are sharp, try using a woodworking tool (or hire a carpenter) to round them off. Just make sure that doing so won't compromise the design. If the piece has any small parts that might fall off or be pried off easily, leave it for someone who doesn't have small children in the home.

Garage sales, swap meets, and artisan fairs can be wonderful sources for secondhand and handmade furniture. Cruise for gently used highchairs, car seats, carriages, and strollers. You might even come across a sweet grandpa-type woodworker whose oak dressers, vanities, side tables, and washstands are beautifully made and reasonably priced. What's more, buying locally means you're cutting down on the transportation required to deliver furniture to market, which, in turn, cuts down on air pollution.

STIMULATING STENCILS

Paint a stencil in the design of your choice just above the baseboards in baby's nursery. It could be a geometric pattern, an argyle pattern, or something more literal, such as leaves or flowers. The higher the color contrast, the greater the appeal.

Besides providing stimulation, a compelling design element located at eye level encourages crawling, which helps your baby build strength, increase physical abilities, boost visual skills, and encourage exploration.

VINTAGE FURNITURE – THE GREENEST OF THE GREEN

Think about it for a minute: vintage furniture has already been manufactured, it's already gone through the off-gassing process, and it's not sitting in the local landfill. That means it's not taxing the planet in any way, making it an environmentally friendly addition to your nursery.

window treatments

Choose vintage-inspired fabrics that have a light feel. Roman shades are a beautiful option, and you can make them your own by adding trim with ribbons or fabric. These shades are available in dozens of styles—from tailored to ruffled, from pleated to plain.

If you're fortunate enough to have a lot of natural light in the nursery, make the windows a strong focal point. Use plantation shutters or wood blinds, layering them with drapes. Combine textiles and textures for an eclectic look, blending two or three muted colors on a single window. Add unique finials to drapery rods for a special touch.

As an aside, I thought I'd share the rule of thumb regarding the required amount of fabric for draperies. To get fullness and complete coverage, the minimum amount of fabric you should buy is one and one-half times the width of the window. For greater fullness, double the window width. For those of you who are lousy at math (and I rank right up there with you), that means a window that is two yards wide would require at least three yards of fabric, and up to four yards of fabric for more dramatic draping.

Stained glass beautifully punctuates a vintage style. Look for an old window at a flea market or antique shop and suspend it from the ceiling in a spot where it will get plenty of natural light. If you're particularly ambitious, pop a hole in the wall and install it as a proper window.

Because of my commitment to safety, I need to throw in a disclaimer here. The colored panels on old stained-glass windows are held in place with lead divider bars. Although lead is not harmful to the skin, it is poisonous if it gets into the bloodstream. To maximize safety, position or hang the window out of baby's reach. Also be sure to wash your hands thoroughly after touching any of the lead parts. Alternatively, look for a window made with copper foil and lead-free solder.

TEENY CREEPY CRAWLIES

Curtains and drapes, like any other fabric, can be home to dust mites. If you use fabric window coverings in the nursery—even if they're made from organic material—frequent launderings are essential.

FLOORING

Hardwood floors lend a lovely vintage look, and are equally stunning in dark, light, and whitewashed finishes. The idea is to give the entire room a feeling of days gone by. If you're lucky enough to have such floors in your home, show them off in all their glory. If not, follow my mantra of "work with what you have."

Regardless of the floor's surface, an area rug in a color that coordinates with your wall palette will give you the soft look you're going for. If you prefer to stick with neutrals, choose carpeting or a rug in a subdued shade—ivory, ecru, beige, honey, peach—that can be a blank canvas for all the colorful toys your child will soon be enjoying.

SIMPLE, SAFE, SAVVY

- Instead of outlet caps, use spring-loaded covers—they snap shut as soon as you take out the plug.

- Invest in baby gates to prevent falls down the stairs and to keep baby from crawling into unsafe spaces. Pressure gates should not be used at the top of the stairs, because they are not permanently affixed to the wall. Use gates with vertical—never horizontal—bars so your little adventurer cannot climb over them.

- Keep your baby monitor turned on whenever baby is in the nursery and you're not.

- Instead of a vaporizer, use a cool-air humidifier. Cool mist is safer because it doesn't carry the burn risk of hot steam. Be sure to clean it regularly to lessen the growth of bacteria and mold.

- Use a bathtub designed especially for infants, with contours and other features designed to prevent baby from slipping under the water.

- Put together a baby first-aid kit.

- Always keep baby wipes and other baby-changing supplies in an easy-to-access spot that your little squirmer can't reach.

- Post emergency phone numbers—police, fire, poison control—next to all telephones in the house.

- Take a class in infant CPR.

BEDDING

This is where you can truly free your imagination. Pull in a fun mix of vintage fabrics, focusing on (safe) trim, bows, ruffles, and decorative touches. (Okay, you might want to leave out the bows and ruffles for a boy, but you can work wonders for both sexes with ribbon stripes.) Use the same idea if you've added a daybed or sofa. Toss decorative pillows on the rocking chair or nursing chair to tie the look together. Needlepoint pillows are an exceptionally nice touch to help define a vintage style.

Don't be shy. Vintage lends itself to a hodgepodge of fabrics and patterns, so go ahead and break loose. As long as your room's design doesn't end up looking like a Victorian bed and breakfast (translation: no wide-brimmed ladies' hats hanging on the wall, please) you'll be fine.

Consider an organic cotton baby hammock as an alternative to a crib. Its gentle embrace and slight swaying motion mimic your baby's experience in the womb, creating an environment that is both familiar and comforting. And when your little one outgrows it, it can be filled with toys, dolls, or stuffed animals.

For the first few months of Felix's life, he slept in a cradle in the master bedroom. We placed a changing table in the corner of the room, making a little "baby nest" not far from our bed. It worked extremely well, and gave us more time to plan the nursery that he would eventually share with his big brother.

A cradle gives a sweet old-world touch to a vintage room. Orbit makes a fabulous bassinet cradle that includes a rocker. All you have to do is dock the bassinet onto the rocker to form a modern cradle, or attach it to the Orbit stroller to form an advanced pram. Another good option is a Moses basket, which can be used until baby is old enough to turn over. It also has the advantage of serving as a great bed away from home when your wee one visits Grandma and Grandpa.

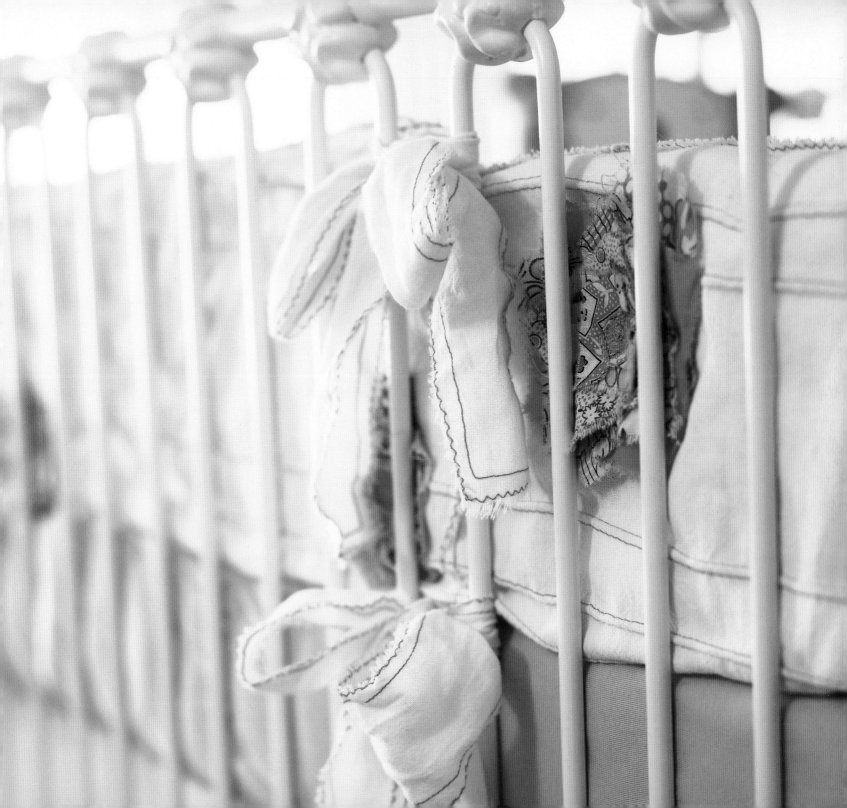

GO WITH GREEN LIGHTS

Replace regular light bulbs with compact fluorescent ones. They use 75 percent less energy, emit less heat, and last ten times longer. If every family in America replaced just one light bulb with an energy-efficient one, enough money would be saved to light more than two and a half million homes for an entire year. As if that weren't impressive enough, it would also prevent greenhouse gases equal to the emissions of almost eight hundred thousand motor vehicles. If you thought one simple change couldn't make a difference, think again!

LIGHTING

Milk-glass lamps are period perfect in a vintage nursery. Look for them at flea markets and antique shops, and buy them in multiples if you find them. While you're scouring through the old stuff, be on the lookout for a lamp base that you like. You can always give it a coat of paint and a new shade to brighten the look.

Chandeliers lend a delightful old-world charm to a vintage-inspired nursery, as do Tiffany-style lamps. Avoid the deeper jewel tones that are most commonly found, opting instead for softer colors that tie in with the overall left-out-in-the-sun feel of the room.

BRING ON THE GIGGLES

An infant's sense of humor develops over time. The more she learns about her world, the more she appreciates the unexpected. When your baby is about six months of age, try introducing toys that make silly sounds. You'll be delighted by the grins and giggles that result.

"Infants experience pleasure from processing information that's a little bit new and a little bit similar."

Paul E. McGhee, PhD, developmental psychologist

GET CREATIVE WITH PLAYTHINGS

Sure, you can spend a small fortune on toys and accessories designed to stimulate your baby's brain, and there's nothing wrong with that if you can afford it. But keep in mind that your little sweet pea has no idea what things cost. (Don't worry—you'll have a chance to deal with pricey designer labels when she's older.) For now, she'll find great intrigue in things like nesting plastic measuring cups, paper-towel tubes, large wooden cooking utensils, and plastic bowls. For physical fun, cut the bottom out of a large box to create a short "tunnel" to crawl through.

Of course, any household items you offer your baby as playthings should be large enough to prevent a choking hazard, free of sharp edges, and safe enough to be gnawed on by little mouths.

See, see.
See Jane.
Oh, see Jane.

special touches

Look for flea market or vintage-inspired whimsical toys to display in baby's room. Old-fashioned wooden playthings generate a sweet nostalgia and are safer than plastic for your little one to handle. Visit craft fairs to find handmade teddy bears sewn from organic materials.

If you have sepia photos of your ancestors, put them in period frames on the dresser. Add a vintage dimension to furniture with tassels or antique hardware, such as doorknobs, dresser knobs, and pulls. Customize the entire look with wallpaper or a small mural that reflects the diffused colors of the room.

Any item that means something to you will make sense in the nursery. One of the nicest things about decorating is that it comes from within, so even if a particular item seems unrelated to your chosen design style, it will still fit in. So don't feel that you have to pack away that modern painting your college room-mate gave you when you went your separate ways after graduation. Don't banish to the attic the slightly askew wooden stepstool your favorite nephew made in first grade and proudly bestowed upon you for your birthday. Put them on display in the nursery right alongside your antique touches and enjoy the memories they evoke.

TOXIC GREENS

Dozens of plants are poisonous to children. The list that follows represents just a few:

Azalea • Daffodil bulbs
Daphne • Delphinium
Dieffenbachia • Foxglove • Holly
Hyacinth • Hydrangea
Lily-of-the-valley • Lupine
Mistletoe • Oleander • Yew
Philodendron • Pyracantha
Rhododendron • Rhubarb leaves

HELPFUL GREENS

While vigilance regarding toxic plants is critical, nature's greens must be given credit for the good they can provide. Denverplants.com has provided the following list of plants that are reputed to remove toxins from the air:

Bamboo palm • Snake plant
Chinese evergreen • Dragon tree
Chrysanthemum • Corn stalk plant
Devil's ivy • Dracaena marginata
Peace lily • Ribbon plant
English ivy • Ficus tree
Gerbera daisy • Spider plant

Just keep in mind that some of these, too, can be poisonous, so check with a nursery to find out. To be perfectly safe, keep all plants out of the reach of little ones.

JUST FOR PARENTS

It's important to have a spot in the nursery where Mom or Dad can settle in to read stories or otherwise connect with baby, and to play dolls or trains, imagine, and have tea parties in later years. This could be a cozy chair or something as simple as a spot on the floor with large pillows. Designating a specific location sets up a tradition that your baby will come to recognize.

Making sure it's a place where you can sit comfortably for extended periods of time is vital, because you don't want to be squirming as the result of tingling limbs or an aching back. This is your time with your baby, and it should be as enjoyable as possible for both of you.

While your little one is still small—prior to the grab-everything-within-reach stage—keep a vase filled with fresh-cut flowers in the nursery. Imagine how special it would be to enter the room and be greeted by the lovely fragrance and the beautiful blossoms!

storage

Baskets with color-coordinated liners are a visually appealing and practical addition, as are bookshelves and an old toy chest. All afford lots of space for essentials and playthings. An old armoire, refinished or stripped and painted with a pickled finish, holds an endless assortment of items—from clothing and diapers to blankets and toys.

Just for fun, line drawers with paper that matches the color scheme of the room. So what if you're the only one who sees them—if they make you smile, that's all that matters.

PUTTING IT ALL TOGETHER
marlo's vintage nursery

It's a girly-girl paradise in a ten-foot by ten-foot space. Marlo's parents wanted her room to be the ultimate in femininity, and their desired look was accomplished with very little pink.

Their home, built in the American Craftsman style, boasts interesting ceiling lines and the original hardwood floors. The idea was to tie the nursery into the vintage charm of the house, working with existing elements as much as possible.

COLOR PALETTE

The nursery's inspiration piece was a scrap of vintage wallpaper in a small harlequin pattern. Marlo's mom collects vintage wallpaper and uses it to create art pieces, so there's an even deeper meaning to her selection. The palette is predominantly coral, with spots of deep plum and ivory. A company called Astek Wallcoverings exactly reproduced the pattern in sheets of new wallpaper that were applied with non-VOC paste (contains no volatile organic compounds).

Astek uses eco-friendly technologies—UV digital printing, screen printing, and solvent-based digital printing—to convert just about any visual into wallpaper. So if you have a drawing, painting, or even a page from a favorite book that you'd like to use to decorate your baby's nursery, the company can turn it into wallpaper or a mural. They also offer an extensive selection of their own wallpapers.

Because the pattern of Marlo's wallpaper makes a strong statement, I opted to use it on only two walls—the window wall and the one opposite it. On the remaining two walls, I used a pale coral paint in a satin finish, accented by bright white on the window frames, molding, and wonderfully wide baseboards. To get a true vintage look, I selected paint from The Old Fashioned Milk Paint Company.

Milk paint is completely nontoxic and environmentally safe. It even has a slightly milky odor when it's first applied, so you know you're working with the real thing. The ingredients are 100-percent natural, and include milk protein, lime, clay, and earth pigments such as ochre, umber, iron oxide, and lampblack. (The lime is alkaline, but becomes totally inert when mixed with the slightly acidic milk.) There's no lead, no chemical preservatives, no fungicides, no hydrocarbons, and no petroleum derivatives, so you and baby can breathe easy.

Milk paint is packaged as a dry powder, so all you have to do is add water to make a pint, quart, or gallon. By altering the thickness of the mixture, you can use it as a full-coverage coat, a wash/stain, or for stenciling. It comes in twenty different colors, which can be mixed to give you a variety of hues and tones. The shades and textures of milk paint truly look like the interior of a home that was built hundreds of years ago, and like its centuries-old counterpart, this milk paint doesn't fade.

HOMEMADE WALLPAPER PASTE

This make-it-yourself recipe is completely natural, works exceptionally well, and is free of pesticides. What more could you want in your baby's nursery?

Ingredients:
1 cup flour (wheat, corn, or rice)
3 teaspoons alum
Water
10 drops oil of cloves (a natural preservative)

Directions:
Combine the flour and alum in a double boiler. (If you don't have a double boiler, make the paste in a smaller pan set inside a bigger one. Fill the larger pan with enough water so it can be brought to a boil without overflowing.) Add water to the flour until the mixture is the consistency of heavy cream. Stir until thoroughly blended. Heat, stirring constantly, until the mixture has thickened to a gravy texture. Let cool. Stir in the oil of cloves. Pour mixture into a glass jar with a screw top. Apply with a glue brush.

Makes 1 cup

Shelf life: Two weeks refrigerated

FURNITURE

To complement the colors on the walls, I selected white reproduction vintage furniture made by PoshTots.com. Pieces include an iron crib with rosettes, a dresser/changing table (the changing pad is easily removed when no longer needed), and a small armoire—the latter two made of painted wood. I also selected a simple wooden side table that was appliquéd to match the PoshTots.com furniture.

The antique-white wooden furniture is softened by a vintage chair and ottoman that were reupholstered in matching fabric. The original chair can best be described as a floral pattern that combined varying shades of baby-poop green, yellow, and brown. Ugly! But the lines are lovely, so I could see its potential. The ottoman started life covered in an old-fashioned brown and yellow print featuring ships, clocks, pitchers, flowers, people, and the Liberty Bell. (I'm sure there's a theme there somewhere, but I've yet to find it.)

I covered both in a floral pattern by Thibaut Design, a company that has been making fabric and wallpaper since the late 1800s. This particular design was screen-printed in England, and combines shades of coral, pink, green, yellow, lavender, and touches of white on a background of soft blue. White piping accents the soft colors. I also had a throw pillow made, which can be moved throughout the nursery to serve a variety of design and functional purposes.

I decided to slightly alter the tailored design of the chair by adding a ruffled skirt to make it look more vintage and feminine. I also painted the wooden legs of the ottoman a bright white to match the trim throughout the room.

WINDOW TREATMENT

An Austrian Roman shade on the four windows—each measuring twenty-one inches wide by almost forty-seven inches long—adds just enough frill without appearing too fussy. Made from eight and a half yards of white linen, it's elegantly full and lush. A white blackout liner hangs behind the shade to allow all light to be filtered out when it's time for Marlo to go to sleep.

The shade was made by a local seamstress found on craigslist.com. I like the idea of employing people within the community whenever possible. It seems to create a sense of old-fashioned togetherness that just can't be duplicated any other way.

FLOORING

The oak floors throughout the house are original, and all it took was some refinishing to bring them back to their former majesty. A large, round, braided cotton rug in coral, green, pink, lavender, and white stands out against the honey-colored wood.

BEDDING

Marlo's bedding was custom made by Natasha Middagh-White, and is named after the designer's daughter, Victoria Mae. Natasha started with a base of 100-percent Egyptian flour-sack cotton, and embellished it by sewing on pieces of exquisite vintage fabric in a flowered design. The flowers are Annie Grace reprints, and some of them are hand-printed with earth-friendly pigments incorporating Natasha's own designs. She uses natural bamboo fiber to fill the bedding, which is naturally antibacterial, offers great breathability, and is not processed with any chemicals. The batting in the quilt is organic cotton. Slender stripes of contrasting threads finish off the design, which picks up all the same colors as the walls, the upholstered furniture, and the rug, making a striking artistic statement.

AWARENESS OF CAUSE AND EFFECT

Too young to speak, but not too young to make cause-and-effect connections? Amazingly, that might be the case. I read about a study performed by a professor of psychology at an East Coast university. She and her colleagues attached one end of a ribbon to a baby's ankle and the other end to a crib mobile. It didn't take long for the babies to discover that kicking caused the mobile to move. Infants as young as six weeks realized this within fifteen minutes, and they increased movement of their feet to make the mobile swing. We've always thought our babies were little geniuses, but I never assumed they were this resourceful!

By the way, if you choose to try this experiment with your baby, I'm sure you realize that you must remain in the nursery throughout the exercise.

LIGHTING

One of the highlights of Marlo's nursery is the magnificent chandelier by Maura Daniel. A reproduction of an antique design, this stunning piece is made of white iron with embellishments of clear beads and faux pearls. If you've already begun the process of decorating your baby's nursery, you'll appreciate the story behind Maura Daniel lighting.

In search of the perfect lamp for their young daughter's bedroom, the husband and wife team of Maura Daniel were disappointed by the lack of design and craftsmanship offered by the lighting industry. Artists in their own right, they decided to create a lighting line that would fill the void. In 1999, they introduced Maura Daniel Lighting Couture, designing fixtures that take decorative indoor lighting to new heights. Their offerings are some of the most beautiful I've seen, and since their selections aren't baby specific, they have the added advantage of growing with your child.

Given the current design of the room, Marlo's chandelier has adorable-baby appeal. As she gets older, it will shift to little-girl sweet. When she's a teenager, it will magically transition to elegant sophistication or radical funk, depending on what the rest of her room looks like.

The table lamp in Marlo's nursery is also by Maura Daniel. About eighteen inches tall, this hobnail milk-glass design features a tulip shade in snow-white silk.

Keep in mind that flea markets are a terrific source for vintage lighting. And the more ornate they are, the more dramatic their statement. Browse for a design you like, and paint it, if necessary, to match your nursery's décor.

SPECIAL TOUCHES

Inspired by the milk-glass table lamp, I went in search of milk-glass vases to match. A six-inch-deep molding shelf wraps around Marlo's room—how I love the practicality and functionality of Craftsman design!—and my plan was to line it with the vases. After wandering from antique store to antique store, I ended up with an impressive collection to display on the shelf.

STORAGE

As every mom knows, the more storage in a baby's room, the better. The top of Marlo's ottoman conveniently opens up to reveal a deep well that can be used to store toys, stuffed animals, or absolutely anything else that might cause clutter. The armoire, although scaled down in size, holds everything from clothing to bedding. Pink wire baskets on the changing table place diapers within easy reach.

POISON CONTROL CENTERS

The national emergency hotline for the American Association of Poison Control Centers is 800-222-1222. You can call this toll-free number twenty-four hours a day, seven days a week to talk to a poison expert.

When you call, you are automatically connected to the poison center for your area. Routing is based on the area code and exchange of the phone number from which you call.

If you call from a cell phone, you will reach either the poison center in the area where you are located or in the home area of your cell phone. Where you land depends on the policy of your cell phone provider. Either poison center can provide you with the care and information you need.

VARIATIONS

Of all the nurseries in this book, Marlo's room is the most gender specific. But in spite of its intense little-girl nature, all it takes are a few simple changes to make it appropriate for a boy or to convert it to gender-neutral.

For a boy, the same wallpaper pattern can be reproduced in blue or green. The remaining two walls could be painted pale blue or soft green, respectively. The existing coral wallpaper could even remain, with the walls painted light blue. If the sex of your baby is going to be a surprise, keep the coral paper and use either lime green or café au lait on the walls, depending on the level of drama you prefer. (I'm guessing you can figure out that lime green is pretty intense, although quite spectacular.)

White furniture works equally well for a boy or girl, but you'll get a more gender-neutral look if you replace the appliquéd style with cleaner, simpler lines. Crisp, white Roman shades on the windows say "boy" or "neutral" more than the scallops on Marlo's very feminine shades. A braided rug will still work, but look for something that picks up the revised color palette of the walls.

The chandelier might be swapped out for something less romantic, such as flush-mounted schoolhouse lighting. The milk-glass table lamp could stay, but I'd suggest replacing the coordinating vases with any type of collection: vintage cars, trains, planes, or old framed sports photos for a boy; wooden blocks, antique toys, or small books for gender-neutral. Some of the artwork tends to look feminine, so it could be replaced with landscapes, scenics, or animals.

ZERO COST, PRICELESS PEACE OF MIND

Taking the necessary steps to help ensure your child's safety is more about common sense and less about expenses:

• Never leave a child unattended in the bath, even in the presence of an older sibling. An excellent rule of thumb is to have one hand on the child the entire time you're bathing her.

• Turn your hot water heater no higher than 120 degrees. A baby's skin is more sensitive than an adult's, so what is warm to us can scald an infant. Always check the water temperature before you put your child in the bath.

• If you live in an earthquake-prone area, do not hang anything on the wall above the crib, since it can fall off onto your sleeping child. (This is sound advice for Mom and Dad's bedroom, too.)

• Wander around your home on your hands and knees, checking out the temptations your baby sees when crawling. You'll probably feel a little weird when you do this, but it could prove to be a surprising eye-opener!

• Keep all hazardous items locked away. Never store anything poisonous in the same place you keep food, because your child will not know the difference.

• Make sure household cleaners, cosmetics, and any poisonous substances are in their original containers, so if baby ingests an unsafe item, you can give accurate information about the ingredients to a poison control center or emergency medical team.

• When you have prescriptions filled, ask for child-resistant containers, but keep in mind that these are not a guarantee of safety. A bright and inventive toddler may be able to outsmart the container if given enough time. The advantage, though, is that the window of time might be enough for you to spot what's going on and intervene.

• Watch out for loose cables and electrical cords. Tie cords up out of reach or bundle them together to remove all slack.

• When cooking, turn pot handles away from the edge of the counter. Use the back burners instead of the front ones whenever possible.

• Since the kitchen is usually a hub of activity, do your best to keep toys and games out of all dining areas.

• Choose a high chair with a wide base to keep if from tipping over. It should also have a harness to keep your little one secure.

• Place an easy-to-spot sticker on your child's bedroom window to alert emergency crews that there might be a child inside. These are often available from your local fire department.

• Keep the following items out of the reach of little fingers: cigarettes, lighters, matches, lit candles, loose change, cell phones, balloons, purses, and diaper bags.

• Always lock doors that lead to areas not intended for children—a home office, guest room, laundry room, and the garage.

• Use window wedges or locks to make sure that all of your windows cannot be opened more than four inches.

Information adapted from Crumb Crunchers Inc. Baby Proofing and Child Safety Consultants

appliquéd Dresser

ONE OF THE BEST THINGS ABOUT VINTAGE DESIGN IS THAT IT LENDS ITSELF TO DOZENS OF DO-IT-YOURSELF PROJECTS. IT'S SO EASY TO ADD A PERSONALIZED TOUCH TO A PIECE OF FURNITURE THAT YOU PICK UP AT A FLEA MARKET OR UNCOVER AT AN ANTIQUE SHOP—AND YOU DON'T HAVE TO BE TEEMING WITH CREATIVITY TO MAKE IT WORK.

One beautiful solution is appliqué, which involves applying composite ornaments (called "compo" in the biz) to a piece of furniture to achieve a completely unique look. This can be done by adhering the ornaments with store-bought glues and/or small nails, but the more traditional method involves steaming. That's the one I've chosen to share with you.

The steaming method I've detailed below may sound a bit daunting, but it's actually very easy and time efficient. Once you lay a few pieces, you'll be an expert. Just give it a try, then give yourself a pat on the back when you realize what a great job you've done.

Gently steaming composition ornaments brings out their full capabilities. The steam's warmth softens the ornament, and its moisture activates a powerful water-based glue within the ornament. The compo then becomes pliable, self-bonding, and moldable to soft curves. If you choose to glue your ornaments, they will be less flexible than if they had been steamed.

Composition ornaments can be purchased in the design of your choice, and are best to work with when they are freshly made. While their beauty lasts forever, their ability to be made flexible and self-adhesive does not. It's all a matter of simple evaporation. Freshly made ornaments contain moistures in the form of water and oils. By nature and design, these moistures will eventually evaporate and the ornament will harden. As this evaporation occurs, flexibility and self-adhesiveness are lost.

The good news is that ornaments can be frozen and stored nearly indefinitely. If you're not planning to use them within about ninety days of purchase, simply wrap them in plastic wrap and put them in the freezer.

My sincerest thanks to the folks at Bomar Designs in Louisburg, Kansas, for providing the information above and for sharing the following directions on how to turn a vintage dresser into a work of art. And just for the record, Bomar is a great source for purchasing ornaments online.

MATERIALS YOU'LL NEED:

- Steaming screen (This is simply a cloth, such as an old sheet, stretched over a wood frame and stapled to the frame.)

- Pan, twelve inches or larger, for holding water (The steaming screen should be made to fit over the pan.)

- Dull knife and thin painter's spatula to pick up the heated ornaments

- X-acto or other sharp knife to cut the heated ornaments

- Portable electric burner or a burner on a stove

STEP-BY-STEP DIRECTIONS:

1) Fill the pan a little less than half full with water. Cover the top of the pan with the steaming screen and heat the water to a low, steady steam. Be careful not to boil the water, because gentle steam is all you need.

2) Determine where you want to place the ornaments. Make sure the surface is free of dust, grease, and dirt.

3) As the water heats and starts to steam, the screen will become wet. A damp steaming screen is important, because the hot moisture activates the glue in the ornaments. It helps to brush the steaming surface with water for additional moisture. This should be done at the start of your project, and then repeated throughout the process as needed. When you have a gentle steam, place one piece of compo, flat side down, on top of the damp steaming screen.

4) Leave the compo on the screen for thirty seconds to two minutes, depending on the thickness and age of the piece. Test the underneath side. If the bottom is wet and slick and the piece is pliable, it's ready. If the compo is not ready, leave it on the steaming screen a little longer. This is a method you do by feel, but after the first piece or two, you'll get the hang of it and the timing will come naturally.

5) When the compo is ready, gently lift it off the screen. Properly warmed compo is sturdy enough to pick up by hand, yet flexible enough to bend without breaking or cracking. Its texture is similar to undercooked pasta, but not as slippery. If you prefer, you can pick up the compo with a thin painter's spatula or dull knife.

6) Position the compo precisely where you want it on your furniture and press it firmly, but gently, into place. Check all the edges to make sure they are pressed down and bonded to the surface. Any compo residue on the furniture or on the ornament can be brushed away with a paintbrush and water.

7) When the compo has cooled and dried, you can paint or finish the furniture any way you choose. Once finished, compo endures for many decades.

8) If you are applying compo to a finished piece or if you want the ornament to have a different finish than the furniture, you can finish the ornament before steaming it and then apply it.

9) All tools and compo residue can be cleaned up with warm water and soap.

NOTES:

If you oversteam the compo and it becomes too soft to handle, remove it from the steam as best you can and lay it design side down, slick side up, to dry and harden. When it's firm again, resteam and start over.

Compo is flexible and easy to cut . Using a very short, strong-bladed knife, you can cut it apart and combine it with other designs to create an original arrangement.

Compo sets very quickly. If necessary, an ornament can be removed with a putty knife within about ten minutes of application. Simply use water to clean the surface where the ornament was applied. The ornament that was removed can be resteamed and used again.

A WORD TO THE WISE

When steamed, compo becomes quite pliable and can be stretched. Take care when applying the ornaments not to stretch them beyond their original size, which could cause slight variations in the layout of your design.

SMART STARTS FOR YOUR BABY

Smart Carrying: Infants who are carried more cry less, and less crying allows more time and energy for growing and learning. The neurological reason is that motion regulates babies. Carried babies show an increase in quiet alertness—a state when they are most content and best able to interact with the environment.

Slings provide the motion and holding that babies need to be neurologically organized. In fact, researchers have reported that carried babies show enhanced visual and auditory alertness. When facing forward in a sling, a baby has a wide view of his environment. He soon learns to choose, focusing on what he wishes to look at and shutting out what he doesn't. This ability to make choices also enhances learning.

Smart Talk: How you talk to your baby has a profound effect on his brain development, and here's where parents—particularly mothers—really shine.

Mothers instinctively use upbeat tones and facial gestures when talking to their babies. They raise the pitch, slow the rate, exaggerate the main syllables, and expressively use their mouths and eyes. How a mother speaks is more important to her baby than what she says.

Mothers also naturally show a brain-building phenomenon called turn-taking. They speak in bursts and pauses, allowing baby the time to process each short, vocal package before the next message arrives. Video analysis of mother-baby communication shows that a mother behaves as if she imagines her baby talking back to her. She naturally shortens

her messages and elongates her pauses to the exact length of time that coincides with the length of the imagined response from the baby. This is her child's earliest speech lesson, which shapes the little one's ability to listen. The infant stores these early abilities and later recalls them when beginning to speak.

You can help facilitate this process in the following ways:

Capture baby's eyes before beginning your conversation. This will enable you to hold his attention longer and increase the likelihood of getting an appreciative response.

Be responsive. To an infant, language is any sound or gesture that makes a caregiver respond to his needs. As he grows, so do his communication tools—facial expressions, body language, gestures, babbles, and eventually, spoken words. By responding sensitively to his cries, you help him refine and develop communication skills.

Address your baby by name. While a baby may not associate his name with himself until later in the first year of life, hearing it frequently triggers a mental association. He learns that this is a special sound he has heard before and that more fun sounds will follow—much as an adult perks up upon hearing a familiar tune.

Keep it lively. Say, "wave bye-bye to the cat" as you direct your wave toward Fluffy. Babies are more likely to recall words that are associated with animated gestures. Give your speech some spark, using inflections at the end of the sentence and exaggerating key words.

Talk about what you are doing. As you go through your daily maintenance tasks of dressing, bathing, and changing baby, narrate what you are doing. While it may feel a bit foolish at first, remember that you're not talking to a stone wall. There is a little person with big ears and a developing brain processing every word he hears.

Smart Responses: How you listen to your baby helps build his brain. A high-response style of parenting promotes brain development by providing the right kind of information at a time when the brain needs the most nourishment.

When researchers evaluated the influence of toys and programs on infant development, mothers still came out on top. Relationships, not things, make baby cleverer.

Smart Music: Music relaxes both the mind and the body. New research is proving what parents have long suspected: music can make infants and children calmer and possibly smarter. The interest in music as a brain stimulant stems from the observations that premature infants in newborn nurseries seem to thrive better when exposed to classical music. Music scientists theorize that music "organizes" the patterns of neurons throughout the brain, especially those associated with creative reasoning. Doctors theorize that music has a calming effect by stimulating the release of endorphins.

Smart Play: To a child, playing and learning are one and the same. Babies learn about their world through play, and parents can learn about what their babies are thinking by watching them play. By observing and sharing in a baby's play, parents can begin to get an idea of all the decision-making and problem-solving processes going on in the baby's developing mind.

Games can stimulate those trillions of brain nerves to make smart connections. Just remember to respect your baby's need to rest from the game now and then.

Two weeks to two months. Facial games are an infant's favorite. When your baby is in the quiet alert state, hold him within the best focusing distance—about eight to ten inches—and slowly stick out your tongue as far as you can. When baby begins to move his tongue, sometimes even protrude it, you know you've registered a hit. Try the same game by opening your mouth wide or changing the contour of your lips, or by copying and exaggerating his expressions. Mirroring is a powerful enforcer of self-awareness. Babies love to mimic your changing facial expressions. Like a dance, you lead and baby follows.

Four months. At this age, babies love games with rattles, rings, rag dolls, and small cuddly blankets. They also love mobiles and other things that dangle, so place them within his reach. Watch him punch at the toy or try to gather it in his arms. Kick toys are another favorite at this age. Pom-poms, rattles, and pleasant noisemakers can be attached to baby's ankles for him to activate with his kicking.

Six to nine months. Balls and blocks are some of the best toys for this stage of life, because babies can do so much with these simple items. Roll games, using foam bolsters, are also very effective. Drape baby over a bolster cushion and place a toy just beyond his reach. Notice how he digs his feet in, pushing and rolling himself forward on the foam cylinder in hot pursuit of the toy.

At this age, babies are becoming curious about the relationship between toys—how a big toy is related to a little toy and how a small object fits into a larger one. This is the stage of container play, where baby can figure out how objects work together—like banging, stacking, and the ever-favorite fill-and-dump.

Nine to twelve months. The mental skill that begins to mature at this age is the concept of object permanence—the ability to remember where a toy is hidden. Try this experiment. Let baby see you place a favorite toy under one of two cloth diapers lying in front of him. Watch him study the diapers, as if figuring out which diaper is covering the toy. By the I'm-thinking expression on his face, you get the impression that he is trying to recall under which diaper the toy is hidden.

Hide-and-seek is a delightful game for your baby. Let him chase you around the couch. When he loses you, peer around the edge of the couch and call him by name. He'll crawl to where he saw you peering, and he'll eventually imitate you by hiding and peeking around the couch himself.

Next, add the game of "sounding." Instead of letting baby see where you are hiding, stay hidden, but call his name. Watch him crawl, and later toddle, around the house in search of the voice he mentally matches with the missing person. Keep sounding to hold the searching baby's interest.

Smart Toys: Interactions, not stuff, build brighter brains. The developmental basis for baby toys is called contingency play, in which baby discovers the cause-and-effect relationship. Basically, a toy should stimulate as many senses as possible, so that baby can see, hear, feel, and do something with the toy.

Here are some fun and inexpensive toys that can stimulate your baby's brain development during the first year:
• Mobiles
• Handheld toys—rattles, rings (three to four inches in diameter), toy telephones, unbreakable mirrors
• Toys that have bright, contrasting primary colors, are black and white, or feature big squares or dots
• Cloth books
• Baby rolls—six-inch foam rubber rollers or cushions that are great props for floor play
• Squeeze and squeak toys
• Blocks and balls
• Grab-and-transfer toys, such as rings

A good toy is one that:
• Fits your child's developmental level
• Encourages imaginative play rather than "doing" something for the child on its own
• Promotes parent-child interaction
• Lasts and grows with your child
• Is safe

Adapted and reprinted with permission from www.askdoctorsears.com

CHAPTER 2

contemporary

"Less is more."

Ludwig Mies
Van Der Rohe,
German architect

In my opinion, there is no true definition of contemporary design, since the meaning changes and evolves with the times. Think about what people called modern in the fifties—today, that style is camp. Think about the psychedelic sixties—today, it's old hippie. Think about the cutting-edge look of the seventies—these days, it's considered retro.

Basically, contemporary design is anything that doesn't fit in anywhere else. It's typified by clean lines, bold graphics, and a complete absence of clutter, with a strong sense of simplicity and clarity. It's light and bright, sleek and fresh, with an airy feel that creates the impression of understated sophistication and open space.

The extreme minimalist look previously equated with contemporary design is a thing of the past. Today's contemporary nursery is warmer and more welcoming—and isn't that the kind of atmosphere you want for your baby?

color palettes

When designing a contemporary nursery, think vivid and playful. This style is ideally suited to a black-and-white accent wall for visual and mental stimulation. Black and white is wonderfully flexible, making a statement when paired with rose or lavender for a girl's room, or with blue or green for a boy's room. Just don't use it with an intense color like China red or New York–taxicab yellow, or the result will be an over-stimulating palette that shouts at you the minute you enter the room. (And just try to generate quiet time in an environment like that!)

If you're not using a black-and-white accent, bright colors are fine — and quite fabulous. Orange is at the top of my list—I love its vibrant energy. But again, don't overdo a color of this intensity, or you might never get baby to relax. If you prefer predominantly white walls in the nursery, consider treating a single wall with graphic details, geometric patterns, or textured wallpaper.

A monochromatic color palette is also very contemporary. Pick a color you like and incorporate it in the nursery in varying shades. For example, paint three walls a pale pinky-violet and the fourth wall a deep plum. Or divide a single white wall into eighteen-inch vertical sections by using one-inch painter's tape, and paint each section a different shade of blue. The white stripes left by the painter's tape will highlight the varying hues.

LOOK AT ME!

Because infants reflexively prefer to look at high-contrast edges and patterns, the use of large black-and-white patterns in baby's room offers the highest possible contrast to the eye, making them particularly appealing. According to research, intense contrast registers more significantly on the retina, sending stronger visual signals to the brain. The result? Greater brain growth and faster visual development—and who doesn't want that for their child?

In addition to black-and-white patterns, infants can also see colored patterns as long as they are not too small and offer high contrast in color and brightness. You can encourage their interest in such patterns with vibrant wallpaper or artwork.

YIPES - STRIPES!

In keeping with your baby's ability to recognize high contrast, stripes are a great way to stimulate vision. Look for dark-and-light patterns in bedding, mobiles, toys, rattles, books—whatever you can find. And at the risk of looking like a jailbird, wear a black-and-white striped shirt now and then and watch your baby focus intently on you.

vibrant orange

chartreuse

plum

blue bird

violet

cool grey

warm grey

pale violet

Furniture

From retro to Eames to a Herman Miller chair, your choices are virtually endless. Choose bold, basic shapes, such as a streamlined crib, a platform bed, or an egg chair. In a contemporary room, less is more.

Whether pieces are straight or curved, look for smooth lines and surfaces. Avoid pieces that are carved, adorned, or embellished. Furniture should not be heavy, so upholstered pieces are an ideal way to soften the entire feel.

You can impart a contemporary look to just about any piece of clean-lined wood furniture by stripping it and painting it to coordinate with the nursery. This is a great way to bring in bright, bold colors without going overboard. So even though your décor is modern, you might want to visit a flea market for an older dresser, crib, or rocking chair whose simple lines can cross over from yesterday to today.

While you're there, look for a sideboard that could work as a changing table. Giving an older piece of furniture an innovative use in your home is both smart and eco-friendly. If you choose a natural wood finish, opt for paler woods with a subtle grain, such as birch, ash, elm, butternut, and maple.

VARIETY—THE SPICE OF LIFE

A broad assortment of textures, shapes, and colors in your baby's room work together to enrich the process of discovery. Appeal to baby's senses with objects that can be touched. While it's great to have compelling things to look at, there's nothing like hands-on play to encourage baby to interact.

SAFETY-FIRST FURNITURE

- Place corner bumpers on furniture to lessen the impact of sharp edges in case baby takes a tumble.

- Make sure your mesh playpen has a small weave (openings less than one-quarter inch), is securely attached, and has no holes in the fabric.

- Measure to ensure that the slats of a wooden playpen are no more than two inches apart. Examine carefully for any loose or missing staples.

- Choose a high chair with both waist and crotch restraining straps that are independent of the tray. If you purchase a folding high chair, look for a secure locking device to prevent it from collapsing.

- If you use a bassinet or cradle, look for a design with a sturdy bottom and a wide base to maximize stability. Legs should have strong locks that will prevent accidental folding while in use.

window Treatments

Because true contemporary design is very streamlined, drapes would not be my first choice here. But as I'll say time and again throughout this book, go with your instincts. If you have your heart set on drapes in a contemporary nursery, by all means, hang them proudly.

If possible, try to customize any fabric treatment on the windows. That way you can use the material you love while having it crafted into something with simple, crisp lines. A one-of-a-kind window covering can really make your contemporary nursery pop.

Solids work well on windows in a contemporary room. Try an accent color that coordinates with the rest of the room, or use white if you prefer a quieter palette. Lined or blackout window treatments, such as Roman shades, are ideal.

SCREENS ARE FOR BUGS

Use window guards and safety netting to prevent falls. Screens prevent bugs from coming in—they do not safeguard against children falling out.

RECLAIM, RECYCLE

When shopping for furniture, look for products made from sustainably harvested or reclaimed wood with a nontoxic finish. Sources of reclaimed wood include old furniture, torn-down houses, and leftovers from other building projects.

Avoid the temptation of inexpensive plywood furnishings, because they can release harmful petrochemical volatile organic compounds (VOCs) into the air.

You can also find stylish furniture made from recycled materials—such as high-grade recycled paper—that are lightweight, surprisingly strong, and trendy. Industrial design students from the National Taiwan University of Science and Technology have created expandable honeycomb paper furniture that is extraordinarily innovative. The honeycomb material is made from recycled paper, and one of the seating designs developed by the students can stretch from one foot to nearly twenty-four. (Too big for the average nursery, but amazing just the same.) Watch for more products like this as their popularity catches on.

FLOORING

Work with what you have, or switch to concrete, cork, bamboo, or natural linoleum. For added warmth, top it with a large shag or low-pile area rug in a natural fiber. Wool is ideal, although it can be expensive. Cotton is a viable alternative, but be sure to use a rug pad underneath it, since its light weight is likely to make it skid across the floor.

Avoid synthetic carpets and rugs, since they go through the process of off-gassing. The resulting chemical odor is toxic, and you don't want a crawling baby in close proximity.

NATURAL FLOORING ALTERNATIVES

Cork floors, which are natural insulators of both heat and sound, are inexpensive, durable, and easy to clean. Better still, they're soft enough to help absorb any bumps baby might experience. They're also naturally antimicrobial, making them beneficial if allergies and sensitivities run in your family. Cork is also a good choice from an environmental perspective, because it reforests itself every six years.

Bamboo floors are stronger and less expensive than most hardwoods, and are also resistant to moisture and stains. The grain resembles that of wood, and the blond color brightens up a room.

Authentic linoleum is made from all-natural materials: sawdust, linseed oils, and pigments, with a jute backing. Soft and easy to clean, it offers the bonus of being available in a variety of colors and patterns to stimulate baby's brain development—a double bonus!

HOMEMADE PLAY DOUGH

Mother Earth News provides this great recipe for making your own nontoxic play dough:

Ingredients:
2 cups flour
1 cup salt
2 tablespoons vegetable oil
2 cups water with several drops of food coloring added*
4 teaspoons cream of tartar

Directions:
Mix ingredients together in a saucepan over medium heat. Stir constantly until mixture thickens. Remove from heat and turn dough onto a plate to cool. Store in a covered container or plastic bag. Finished creations can be baked slowly in the oven until hardened, then painted.

* You can also add vegetable juices or mashed up vegetables—such as carrots, beets, or spinach—for color instead of food coloring.

BEDDING

Baby's bedding just might be the source of your color inspiration. DwellStudio offers a great selection of modern graphic designs—they're decorative, minimal, and fresh. Bright solids also work well in a contemporary setting. The important thing is to keep it simple. Elements such as bows and ruffles have no place here.

Choose fabrics that will help balance the starkness of the furniture. If you can't find anything that stirs your soul, buy fabric you love and have the bedding custom made. The important thing is not to feel that you must have all elements perfectly coordinated, with matchy-matchy sheets, quilt, and bumper. Play with different solids. Experiment with pattern mixes. I promise you—your baby will love whatever you come up with.

BRAVO FOR BAMBOO

It's furniture...it's flooring...and it's also bedding and clothing. That's bamboo's claim to fame, and it's an excellent resource to tap for your baby.

The fiber boasts a host of benefits:

• Soft, natural sheen that's silky to the touch

• Moisture-wicking and breathable to keep baby comfortable

• Naturally antibacterial to fight odors

• Naturally hypoallergenic for sensitive skin

• Natural protection against UV rays

• Easy to care for—just toss in the washer and dryer

• Eco-friendly

• 100-percent biodegradable

Bamboo is used to make blankets and crib sheets—even onesies, hats, socks, and an assortment of clothing for baby.

Information courtesy of babybambu.com

WHERE THERE'S SMOKE...

• Use smoke detectors throughout your home, and install a carbon-monoxide alarm outside the nursery. Check the batteries regularly.

• Have a fire extinguisher on hand.

• Plan a fire escape route with all members of your family.

• Eliminate access to fireplaces, woodstoves, space heaters, and radiators with a screened barrier.

LIGHTING

In any style nursery, the lighting should reflect the lines of the furniture. If you decide to go contemporary, the simple rounded shape of a drum shade coordinates beautifully with just about any clean-lined table lamp. In fact, I'll go out on a limb and say that even an ornate or quirky vintage base can be toned down and given a more contemporary look by pairing it with a simple shade. If the base is super fussy—but you absolutely love it or it has strong sentimental value – give it a coat of paint to tie it in with your color palette and quiet the visual screaming.

Streamlined wall sconces work well, too—buy them in pairs—or opt for the distinctive statement afforded by a bold arc lamp. Recessed and track lighting add a modern touch and offer great flexibility when put on a dimmer switch. Best of all, they blend in with the ceiling and seem to disappear, offering just the right amount of light without any space-occupying intrusion.

SPECIAL TOUCHES

Find a mobile that you love, incorporating the lively colors you've chosen for the nursery. Add modern art in vivid tones to the walls. A coffee-table art book is a great source of inexpensive photos. Rotate the gallery every few months to keep the intrigue fresh.

Linear shelves add a wonderful touch to a contemporary nursery. Paint them a primary color and hang them on a light or neutral wall for the high contrast that babies love.

Black and white photos can be very modern when used in groupings. Go for sets of nine to twelve, and change them periodically to satisfy baby's growing curiosity. When she's old enough to start creating artwork of her own, replace the photos with her drawings.

IT'S A BIRD...IT'S A PLANE...IT'S...WHAT IS THAT ANYWAY?

Often overlooked and entirely underestimated, the ceiling is an important part of the nursery's overall design. Think about it for a minute: babies spend their early months on their backs, so why not provide something intriguing to look at from that angle? And once their full depth of field develops at about eight months, a crib mobile is no longer enough – nor is it safe when baby can push himself up and grab it.

To lend true brain-stimulating punch to the ceiling in baby's room, work with both color and dimension. Cut shapes out of plywood, paint them a color that contrasts with the ceiling, and suspend them a few inches from the ceiling. You can use eyebolts that are screwed into both the cutouts and the ceiling, joined by sturdy wire or a small chain. The result is a geometric art gallery that will catch baby's eye and capture his curiosity.

arranging PHOTOS

If you're using primary colors in your décor, consider purchasing inexpensive wooden frames and painting them in bright, coordinating hues. Alternatively, inexpensive metal frames are available in a variety of colors. Choose mattes to match or complement: an orange matte with an orange frame…a yellow matte with a blue frame. The vivid tones will set off black and white photos beautifully, and they'll give you a unifying theme to tie your wall display together.

The designer's rule for hanging photos is to place them at eye level. Of course, eye level for a six-foot-three man is not the same as for a five-foot-four woman, but the average measurement is fifty-seven inches from the floor to the center of the photo. You can use this as the starting point for your largest or favorite photo, then position the rest of the photos around it.

Beyond that simple rule of thumb, don't feel that you have to employ math when planning your arrangement. Loosen up. If you want to keep it simple, go with two or three rows of photos assembled in straight horizontal lines, trying to keep the centermost part of the display at eye level. Or get a bit free-form and group photos tightly—just a couple of inches between them—into a single, unified shape.

Start by arranging artwork on the floor, or cut templates out of paper in the size and shape of all your frames and tape them to the wall. This will give you a clear idea of what your final display will look like. Then play. Move things around. When you like the way it looks, start hammering nails.

If you'd prefer not to put a lot of little holes in the wall, go for a few larger holes and hang shelves instead. Displaying your framed photos in this way makes it easy to rotate the gallery whenever you choose.

Hanging items from the ceiling is said to be good feng shui. Paper Japanese cranes work well, and can be found in patterns and in metallics. Dream catchers —reputed to catch bad dreams in their delicate webs—are another good choice.

I recently designed a nursery where one wall was painted a deep cobalt blue. I used sidewalk chalk to write "Twinkle, twinkle, little star" in cursive near the top of the wall, then hung a large, decorative star from the ceiling. A chalkboard provides an easy way for your little artist to give flight to his imagination and creativity. Buy a framed one from an art-supply or school-supply store, or use chalkboard paint to make your own.

storage

Plastic and felt bins work exceptionally well with contemporary design, adding a colorful component while keeping toys out of sight. Another good choice is modular shelving—try a little bit of creativity to give them a custom look. Add your own corbels beneath them to give the illusion that they're supporting the shelves. Arrange rows of shelves in a corner. Stagger them. Hang them side by side. Go for a one-of-a-kind design. Their modular nature gives you the freedom to experiment until you find a configuration you like.

Hanging shelves and bookshelves always offer excellent storage, and will maintain the clean-lined integrity of your contemporary nursery as long as they're not overly filled with clutter. Make use of the space under baby's crib to stash items you'd prefer to have out of sight. For small items like stuffed animals, dolls, and wooden toys, use an over-the-door compartmentalized hanging bag designed for shoes.

PHTHPHTHPHTH ON PHTHALATES

Phthalates (pronounced thah-lates) are chemical compounds that turn rigid plastic into pliable plastic, making toys—like your little one's favorite rubber bath-tub duckie—more flexible. They're also commonly used in teething rings, which means they often find their way into baby's mouth.

Over time, phthalates leech out of the plastic and into the air. They can also be absorbed by the skin via direct contact. Studies on lab animals show that some phthalates interfere with the production of testosterone and cause malformed sex organs. There is much controversy on the substance, but the better-safe-than-sorry adage applies here.

Before you offer baby any object that will be chewed on or sucked on—which means just about any-thing—make sure it's completely devoid of chemicals. See the Vendors and Resources section at the end of this book for a list of manufacturers of nontoxic toys.

PUTTING IT ALL TOGETHER
pearson's contemporary nursery

Pearson and her parents live in a contemporary home, so it was only natural that her ten-foot by twelve-foot nursery would follow the same design.

The inspiration piece for the room was bedding made by DwellStudio. When Pearson's mom was pregnant, she did what most moms-to-be do: she pored over every baby and decorating magazine she could find in search of ideas for her baby's nest. Her quest led her to the bedding, which virtually popped off the page and screamed, "I'm the one! Pick me!" There was no doubt that the nursery's design would revolve around this beautiful fabric.

That's the great thing about inspiration pieces—you land on them with complete conviction. I've never worked with a parent who was hesitant or ambivalent about the item that was chosen to get the entire design process started. Whether it's something sentimental or something you find while shopping for your unborn baby, you absolutely know it when you see it.

COLOR PALETTE

Playing off the bedding colors, I painted Pearson's walls an ash brown. Like Marlo's vintage nursery, Pearson's room features paint by The Old Fashioned Milk Paint Company. The color is a marriage of brown and gray in a satin finish —changing with the light at different times of day, shifting from cool to warm and back again.

If brown seems to you like an unusual choice for a baby's room, I encourage you to rethink the color. Brown is a fabulous neutral that serves as the ideal backdrop for more vivid shades. The walls of Pearson's nursery make the turquoise used in the rug and the ceiling take on a life of its own.

Ah, the ceiling! This is one of my favorite parts of this nursery. Since babies spend so much time on their backs, it makes perfect sense to spruce up the area overhead to give them something interesting to look at.

A company called Talissa Décor makes the polystyrene ceiling tiles I selected for Pearson's room. Embossed to create a three-dimensional effect, they're designed to look like tin architectural tiles. Each square tile measures a bit less than twenty inches by twenty inches, and they're feather light and easy to install—no special skills or professional tools required. They're the best possible choice for old stucco (popcorn) ceilings, because there's no need for any preparation work prior to installation. Just attach them with nontoxic glue and you're done!

Dozens of patterns are available, so have fun deciding which one you like best. You can choose from Talissa Décor's selection of colored tiles, or you can purchase them in white and paint them in the color of your choice, which is the option I decided on. Simply use a good-quality, solvent-free latex or acrylic paint and apply it with either a roller or a spray gun. As an added bonus, the tiles are waterproof and moisture-proof, they will not mildew or rot, they're easily cleaned with just soap and water, and they're completely recyclable when you tire of them. Best of all, they can transform the image of your nursery in a single day—just like they did in Pearson's room.

The baseboards, crown molding, and all trim were painted with a white semigloss—the best finish for trim. An extra coat of paint was added to the baseboards for maximum color saturation and durability.

FURNITURE

All the earth-friendly, wooden furniture in this contemporary nursery is from Netto Collection. The Loft crib, made in cherry-stained ash and white lacquer, features a mattress platform and fixed side rails. The recessed storage drawer has brushed stainless-steel pulls. The crib mattress is made of organic cotton and wool.

This particular crib is available with a daybed conversion kit, which allows it to grow with your child and serve down the road as a toddler bed, then a sofa. Pearson's family liked the idea of expanded use, so I added it to the mix.

The matching Loft dresser doubles as a changing table. The pad sits on top of the dresser and is attached to the wall with special straps, so there's no risk of slippage. It also has a safety belt so Pearson can be buckled in for added security. Another option is to attach the changing pad to the top of the dresser with industrial velcro. While it's a bit messy to

install, this solution is very effective.

A streamlined wooden bookshelf attaches to the wall and frees up much-needed floor space. Also by Netto, it's finished in a high-gloss white paint.

Netto first introduced modern baby furniture in 2003, expanding young parents' options by offering contemporary style for kids' rooms. The company has grown to release four collections and CUB, its new mid-priced line. Products combine simplicity of design with solid construction, so there's no reason why this furniture ever has to be thrown away.

One of the things that impresses me the most about this European company is its environmental statement: "Netto Collection sees the health of our children as inseparable from the health of our planet, and we care deeply about both. We use only sustainably harvested wood. All our composite materials meet the stringent European 'E1' toxicity standards. Our finishes are nontoxic and non-VOC emitting." That's the kind of furniture I want to put in the nurseries I design.

The glider and matching ottoman are by Monte Design, a Canadian company. The style I decided upon is Luca, and I chose it in a neutral color called stone, accented by brown piping and a deep brown—stained maple wood base. The suede microfiber is water-repellant and stain-resistant—soft to the touch and extremely durable. A smooth gliding mechanism on both pieces makes this the ultimate nursery pair.

The wing-style glider features simple lines—that's precisely what you want in a contemporary nursery—and promises a commitment to Mom's comfort. The ergonomic arm height is just right for feeding baby, the high back provides a great head rest, and the removable lumbar pillow affords the option of extra back support. And, of course, the gliding motion means soothing comfort for both mother and baby. Whether Pearson and her mom are snuggled together for a middle-of-the-night feeding, an afternoon story, or some anytime cuddling, this chair and ottoman will be their haven.

I also selected a coordinating bassinet called Ninna-Nanna, with a removable basket that nestles into a dark brown, solid wood rocker base. The bassinet's padded sides are covered by a removable and machine-washable suede microfiber—the same stone-colored water-repellant and stain-resistant fabric as on the chair and ottoman. Monte Design includes a waterproof mattress and two fitted sheets with this purchase.

While this bassinet won't be used in the nursery, it's the perfect piece of furniture to keep in the master bedroom when Pearson's parents want her close. Measuring thirty-four inches long by twenty-four inches wide by twenty-eight inches high, it takes up little space beside Mom and Dad's bed and serves an infinitely useful purpose.

Originally, my plan was to buy a simple white side table to place beside the glider. At the last minute, I happened upon a tree-trunk table that completely broke the contemporary mold of the room. Made entirely of wood and carved to look like a tree, it measures seventeen inches in diameter and seventeen inches tall. I found this unique piece quite by accident, and was intrigued by its look that falls somewhere in the realm of primitive-modern, nature-inspired, and fun-contemporary. (See what I mean about design crossing over from one style to another?) However you define it, it adds an unexpected touch of whimsy to the otherwise cutting-edge nursery. The bonus feature is the fact that the trunk opens up to reveal spacious storage inside—a benefit that I would not have gotten from a basic side table.

The addition of this piece reflects one of my design philosophies: don't be afraid to shift direction a bit and toss in something totally different. If it's pretty, practical, or just plain appealing; if it's fun, frivolous, or fittingly functional; if you simply feel that you and your baby just can't live without it…make it yours.

WINDOW TREATMENT

The window in Pearson's room sits high on the wall. Because of limited space and the drama of the ceiling, I wanted the window treatment to be relatively simple and unobtrusive.

I chose a clean-lined Roman shade in crisp 100-percent linen, keeping things natural and earth-friendly. The eggshell color matches the background of the bedding, and the four-inch banding of turquoise around the sides and bottom of the shade ties in with the ceiling, the rug, and the crib bumper.

FLOORING

The original plan was to remove the carpeting in Pearson's nursery and replace it with eco-excellent bamboo flooring. After all, it doesn't get much better than bamboo when you're trying to tread lightly on the planet. In addition, the previous owners of the house told Pearson's parents that the floors in that room were in bad shape, so replacement made good sense.

Or not. When the carpeting was ripped out, not-so-bad floors were revealed—much to the surprise and delight of the family. With an eye on cost-efficiency and a sense of waste-not responsibility, they sanded the existing floors and finished them with a cherry stain to match the rest of the house. (Pearson's pregnant mom stayed away from the room throughout the process.)

Never underestimate the power of a spectacular area rug. To soften the wood floors, I added a five-foot by eight-foot 100-percent New Zealand wool rug called Lulu, designed by Angela Adams and named for one of her favorite cats. She refers to the color as "pool," and it is essentially the same shade as the turquoise used on the ceiling and in additional touches throughout the room. The field is cut pile with loop circles in a darker shade of blue, imparting a great multidimensional look.

Angela Adams' designs are best known for their sense of timelessness, simplicity, and balance. Her patterns are inspired by the natural beauty of life off the coast of Maine, where she has made her home. In her words, "My style is very natural. I hand-draw everything in a sketchbook and

I'm not very technical or perfect, so I rarely use straight lines or measured patterns. I can get inspired by a mud puddle or footprints in the snow. Someone standing in front of a yellow school bus in a green shirt can inspire a whole color palate for a season."

To me, her work reflects the natural approach I try to take with every room I decorate, particularly a nursery. Gentleness, integrity, a humble appreciation for the beauty that exists in our world; these are qualities that I want my children—and all children—to remember and embrace.

WHAT'S IN *YOUR* BABY LOTION?

When the Environmental Working Group (EWG), a nonprofit environmental research organization based in Washington, DC, evaluated more than a thousand children's body-care products, the group's studies revealed several chemicals that had not been assessed for safety and others that were known to cause cancer. While some pediatricians see a link between these chemicals and health problems, manufacturers claim that the safety of their products has been substantiated.

While the jury is still out on this critical matter, safeguard your baby by outfitting the nursery with washes, lotions, shampoos, and other personal-care items that are free of fragrance, dyes, and preservatives.

For more information, visit www.ewg.org.

BEDDING

Pearson's DwellStudio bedding is called Charlotte, and it combines shades of ash brown, bright fuchsia, lime green, and turquoise on a neutral eggshell background. The crib bumper features large blocks of a damask-type pattern in all four colors. The tailored, no-fuss crib skirt is striped in ash and eggshell, with a striped blanket to match. These were paired with a solid aqua fitted crib sheet.

For those of you who might not be familiar with DwellStudio, the company began in 1999 and has grown to become a much sought-after source for décor for the minimal home. DwellStudio's claim to fame includes a unique sense of color, an unwavering commitment to quality, and a strong focus on remaining a step ahead of the crowd.

In an effort to bring modern textile design to the world of bedding, DwellStudio quickly established itself as a leader and innovator in the bedding market. On the baby front, it has received high accolades for bedding in printed, solid, and sateen styles rendered in modern, urban designs.

LIGHTING

The old-fashioned dome ceiling fixture in Pearson's room was replaced by a pendant lamp designed by Maura Daniel. A blend of chrome and clear crystal spheres makes a brilliant statement that seems to me to be part modern, part vintage. I added a turquoise drum shade to match the ceiling—and the bulb, of course, is an energy-saving one.

SPECIAL TOUCHES

As you'll often hear me say in this book, mirrors are a great solution to visually expand a room, especially when hung on a wall opposite a window. Pearson's parents received a funky starburst mirror as a wedding present—one of those items they couldn't quite decide if they love or hate. It's definitely an imposing creation, measuring thirty-five inches in diameter when you factor in the chrome rod-and-disk spokes. After moving it from room to room over the years —and not particularly liking how it looked anywhere—they finally found the perfect home for it in Pearson's nursery.

Artist and dear friend Nancy Hadley made the wall hanging of a large, wispy, white feather with the words "La Plume" lettered above it. After all, it's never too early for Pearson to learn to speak French.

STORAGE

Netto offers a line of storage baskets that are perfect for toys and quick cleanups. Made of ivory felt, they measure eleven inches high by seventeen inches wide by seventeen inches long. Netto also makes fabulous linen boxes. They're only seven inches high—and a whopping twenty-five inches long and sixteen inches wide—making them the perfect size for storing under the crib. The built-in drawer under the crib is the ideal spot for blankets, while the dresser drawers hold additional linens and diapers.

Pearson's closet was literally an empty shell—not a rod or a shelf in sight. I hired Closets to Go to customize this blank canvas to meet the needs of a little one's storage. The result was done all in white to match the furniture and the molding—a combination of hanging rods and drawers for clothing; open shelves for blankets, diapers, and additional clothing and accessories; and wire bins at floor level for toys—placing them within easy reach for when Pearson can crawl.

Given all this storage space, the room is very uncluttered with few visible toys.

VARIATIONS

Pearson's room has the advantage of being very gender-neutral—from the color palette to the furniture to the accessories—so no changes would have to be made for a boy.

BRAIN STIMULATION: BENEFICIAL – AND EASY

There's no such thing as firing up your baby's brain too early. According to Robert F. Newby, PhD, pediatric neuropsychologist and Associate Professor of Neurology in the Medical College of Wisconsin Department of Neurology, "Technically, the brain is being stimulated from conception on. A mother's diet, self-care, and avoidance of toxins all contribute to the development of the nervous system and naturally help to stimulate the brain."

Best of all, brain stimulation is not a difficult thing to do. Dr. Newby goes on to say, "Touch, hearing, sight—all the infant's senses can be stimulated by very simple methods. It's a myth that high-tech gadgets are needed to stimulate a child's brain. Talk to the child, play with the child, hold the child, comfort the child, and meet his or her physical and psychological needs in a timely manner. That's really the main thing that's needed."

"I think that I see something deeper, more infinite, more eternal than the ocean in the expression of the eyes of a little baby when it wakes in the morning and coos or laughs because it sees the sun shining on its cradle."

Vincent Van Gogh

one-of-a-kind lamp

YOU CAN CREATE YOUR OWN CUSTOM LIGHTING WITH A COAT OF PAINT AND A BIT OF FABRIC THAT COORDINATES WITH YOUR NURSERY'S DÉCOR. START WITH AN INEXPENSIVE GLAZED CERAMIC LAMP FROM A THRIFT SHOP OR DISCOUNT STORE. LOOK FOR LINES THAT YOU LIKE, EVEN IF EVERYTHING ELSE ABOUT IT—THE COLOR, THE LAMPSHADE—MAKES YOU CRINGE. (YOU MAY HAVE TO PUT ON YOUR IMAGINATION HAT, BUT IT WILL BE WELL WORTH IT.) YOU'LL BE THE ONLY MOMMY ON YOUR BLOCK WITH THIS ONE-OF-A-KIND DESIGN, AND YOU'LL BE ABLE TO BRAG THAT YOU DID IT YOURSELF!

When shopping for a new lampshade, keep in mind that a cylindrical shape is the easiest to work with. A dome shape, with different top and bottom diameters, just takes a bit more work and patience.

Note that I'm recommending the use of an airbrush or spray gun loaded with non-VOC latex paint instead of a can of spray paint. That's because the latter contains petroleum solvents, which you don't want to use in your baby's room. If you can find environmentally friendly pump-spray (nonaerosol) paint, by all means feel free to use it.

MATERIALS YOU'LL NEED:

- Lamp
- Sandpaper or steel wool
- Non-VOC latex paint
- An airbrush or spray gun
- Plain white lampshade
- One-half to two yards of decorative fabric, depending on the size of the shade
- Pencil

- Scissors
- Ruler
- Craft glue or fabric glue
- Ribbon, braid, or any other trim—either solid or patterned

STEP-BY-STEP DIRECTIONS:

1) Remove the shade and cord from the lamp.

2) Carefully rough up the glazed surface of the lamp using sandpaper or steel wool.

3) In a well-ventilated area, paint the base of the lamp in the color of your choice. Several coats may be needed.

4) Set aside to dry completely.

5) When dry, reattach the cord.

6) Lay the fabric, right side down, on a large table or work surface.

7) Place the lampshade on its side on the fabric, starting near a corner of the material.

8) Using a light pencil stroke, mark the fabric along the top and bottom edges of the shade.

9) Slowly roll the shade over the fabric, marking the material about every inch where it comes in contact with the top and bottom of the shade.

10) Keep doing this until you reach your first marks, then add another three or four inches of extra fabric.

11) Cut the fabric along your marked lines.

12) Carefully apply fabric glue to the lampshade.

13) Starting at the seam of the shade, begin to attach the fabric. Smooth and stretch it as you go to prevent any wrinkles and puckers.

14) Continue until you get to the seam where you started. Fold the edge under and glue in place.

15) If any fabric overhangs the top or bottom edge of the shade, trim it with scissors.

16) To add the finishing touch to your shade, glue ribbon or braid along the top and bottom edges. Leave a little extra so you can fold it under before gluing it down. If you prefer, you can use wider ribbon and fold it over the top and bottom edges, gluing it down on both the inside and outside to keep it in place.

17) At this point, you can stop or keep going. You can glue anything you choose to the lampshade—such as sequins or beads—or stencil a design onto the fabric.

CHAPTER 3
traditional

"Be faithful to
your own taste, because
nothing you really like is
ever out of style."

Billy Baldwin, American
interior decorator

Traditional design is best defined as classic Americana. All you have to do is flip through the pages of a Pottery Barn catalog or stroll through the Ralph Lauren section of your favorite department store to get a taste of what this style is all about.

Think understated elegance. Think classic East Coast manor homes. Think of the styles of the 18th and 19th centuries. Traditional design has evolved over the years, moving out of the realm of stuffy and old-fashioned and into a fresher, more exciting interpretation.

Essentially, traditional design is all about finely crafted wood pieces—Queen Anne, Chippendale, Thomas Sheraton. But before you start rolling your eyes anticipating huge price tags on furniture, let me add that there are scores of less expensive—and okay, less authentic—interpretations out there that will serve your purpose quite wonderfully.

When designing your traditional nursery, put yourself in the place of your child. Start from the floor up—after all, that's where baby will spend most of his first several months. Wainscoting, beadboard, wide baseboards, and chair rails are beautiful touches in a classic room, creating an ageless, enduring look.

When raising your sights higher, you can lend instant traditional charm to the nursery with different types of decorative wall molding. Options include ceiling molding, which goes between the wall and the ceiling; base molding, which goes between the wall and the floor; and door and window molding, which goes between the door/window and the wall. Countless patterns are available, so you can choose whichever style you like the best. Select contrasting wall and molding colors if you want the molding to pop, or keep the shades of similar intensity for a more understated look.

color palettes

Perhaps the simplest and most effective way to determine the color scheme for your traditional nursery is to look out the window. After all, have you ever met a child who wasn't obsessed with the outdoors? My son Oliver would live in the yard if we let him. And I know a couple who took their three-year-old daughter on vacation to Costa Rica, where Katelyn spent most of her time on the ground, enchanted by the local bugs. Mother Nature is a child's first best friend—well, next to Mommy, of course—and her voice rings loud and clear in a traditional nursery. It just makes good decorating sense to invite her inside.

Whether decorating for a girl or a boy, use the blue of the sky, the green of the grass and trees, the soft yellow of the early-morning sun. To add a feminine touch, accent with spots of blossom pink. If you're in a position to do so, hire an artist to bring the outdoors indoors by painting a mural of something found in nature: a flowering branch, a garden scene, birds, baby animals, or anything else you and your little one would like.

If the view outside the nursery includes a dogwood tree, paint a companion tree on baby's wall. If you live in a big city, balance the tall buildings that punctuate the skyline with a bit of the countryside: a graceful willow tree beside a brook, a vegetable patch (is that a bunny hiding behind the cabbages?), a cluster of purple irises. The possibilities are endless, so just go where your imagination takes you.

You might even find bedding or wallpaper that leads the way and defines your color palette. If fabric serves as your inspiration piece, cut out a section and stretch it over canvas or frame it to hang on the wall.

BRUSHES AND ROLLERS AND PAINT, OH MY!

- Do not paint while you are pregnant. The fumes could be harmful to you and your unborn child.

- Paint at least one month before the baby sleeps in the room. You want to be sure to eliminate all traces of the odor.

- If any paint was applied before 1978, remove it. Paint used prior to that year could contain lead, which is very hazardous to children.

blossom

soft sky

grape

orange

sprout

iris

farmhouse red

grass green

sunshine

THE IMPACT OF COLOR

Color has a strong influence on our lives, affecting our moods, emotions, attention, and ability to learn. For centuries, it has also been considered to have significant healing properties. Parents usually choose colors for their child's nursery that reflect their own personalities. However, it's a good idea to put some extra thought into selecting the room's palette, since it just might have an impact that goes far beyond aesthetics.

Infants cannot see true color at birth, and recognition of primary shades begins to develop at two to four months of age. Newborns can distinguish bright colors, large shapes, and bold patterns. They prefer contrasting dark-and-light patterns versus solid colors. They can also distinguish light and movement, but they can focus only on objects eight to twelve inches away. Vision is fully developed by about eight months.

Initially, stationary crib mobiles in high-contrasting patterns or bright shades of red, green, blue, and yellow will help develop focus. At about two months of age, babies lose interest in stationary objects and prefer to track moving objects, so a spinning mobile is beneficial to help develop attention. Other attention-improving options include brightly colored toys and pictures on the wall.

Color impacts everyone differently, but each color exhibits specific qualities.

red

A strong and passionate color, red increases energy and enthusiasm, generates excitement, and instills confidence. Its healing properties are associated with energizing all organs and systems, including the heart, blood circulation, and the senses of hearing, smell, taste, vision, and touch.

Because of the intense qualities of the color, red is recommended as an accent—not the primary color—in a child's room. Since it is not a calming color, it can cause problems when trying to get a child to settle down to rest, or even to play for extended periods of time. However, research shows that an occasional bold stroke of red or orange attracts a child's attention to details.

orange

A cheerful color, orange is bold, daring, exciting, and spontaneous. It creates a sense of adventure, encourages confidence and independence, and takes creativity and enthusiasm to new levels.

From a healing standpoint, orange stimulates the lungs, respiration, and digestion. It is great for new mothers beginning to breast-feed, as it is reputed to increase milk production and boost the appetite. According to research studies, the use of colors such as orange and red may elevate IQ by as much as twelve points.

green

Abundant in nature, green is said to be the most refreshing color and the easiest on the eyes. It brings peace, rest, hope, comfort, balance, and harmony, creating a feeling of safety and security within a family.

A soft shade of green is good for preemies or infants with gastroesophageal reflux syndrome. Because it is said to strengthen and preserve eyesight, it may be a good color choice for an infant with retinopathy of prematurity or simply to help develop stronger vision in all infants. Green has been known to alleviate depression, nervousness, and anxiety, so it is a beneficial nursery color for first-time moms or those who are prone to postpartum depression.

blue

Because blue is the color of the sky and the ocean, it is perceived as a constant in our lives, and therefore soothing to us. Calming, tranquil, and peaceful, it may encourage individuals to be trustworthy, committed, and dependable.

Blue is an excellent choice to help calm and prepare a baby for sleep and to relax a little one with colic, and is often used to help babies with respiratory distress syndrome. Additional health benefits include blue's ability to decrease the heart rate, making it useful for premature infants with cardiac problems. Children with a history of jaundice have been successfully treated with blue lights.

black

A submissive color, black makes a large room appear smaller. The result is a cozy, stabilizing feeling that anchors the room and promotes a sense of being grounded. What's more, it strengthens the ability to focus and gain a sense of self in space.

white

A pure and joyous color, white symbolizes cleanliness and new beginnings. It aids in clear thinking and encourages clarity, generating a sense of balance and harmony. It is said that placing white on any part of the body that requires healing is the fastest way to bring about health to the affected area. In addition, white is a common color to treat depression.

yellow

Do you ever wonder why cautionary road signs are yellow? That's because it's the most visible color for our eyes to see. Yellow is a warm and sunny hue that sparks optimism, enlightenment, energy, and creativity. It stimulates mental activity and memory, and is said to encourage expression and communication.

From a therapeutic perspective, yellow is believed to heighten mentality and strengthen muscles. As your child gets older, yellow can assist in concentration, memorization, visualization skills, speaking, and writing, which is why it is commonly used in schools.

Because it is only fair to present both sides, some research studies have shown that babies cried the most in yellow rooms, opera singers threw more tantrums in yellow dressing rooms, and couples argued most in yellow kitchens – one more reason why I encourage you to gather information and make your own choices.

purple

A rich, uplifting color, purple provides a sense of calmness to the mind. It promotes inner strength and inspires creativity and artistic talents, and is associated with respect and spirituality. From a healing standpoint, purple may help calm a colicky baby and foster peaceful sleep. It also provides a soothing effect on the ears, eyes, and nervous system.

pink

Sweet, calming, and innocent, pink symbolizes youthfulness and softness. It is often associated with kindness, and is said to help heal sadness and allow individuals to get in touch with their feelings.

brown

Because of brown's deep connection to the earth and its natural and organic components, it is believed to afford a sense of stability and wholeness. It is a very grounding color, providing a feeling of order, reliability, and protection.

Source: Kari Thompson, OTD, OTR/L, BCP, SWC, CLE, CID

Furniture

In keeping with the signature component of traditional design, hardwoods are a great choice for baby's room, particularly if they have a dark stain. A rich cherry is elegant and one of my absolute favorite woods, especially in a sleigh crib. Try to find a gently used one, or start dropping hints if you have a friend or family member who's about to retire one. Don't be afraid to mix different types of wood, because you don't want the nursery to look staged for an *Architectural Digest* photo shoot. In fact, this rule applies to any decorating design you choose. This is your baby's room; this is your home; and the point is for it to feel — and look — lived in.

If a sleigh crib isn't your style, consider a four-poster crib with or without a canopy. If you purchase a used one, be sure to check all parts to ensure that they're safe. Look for solid, timeless pieces with decorative molding or painted accents. The traditional nursery isn't the place for simple, clean lines, so have fun with something more ornate.

Substitute a sideboard for a changing table. With a few modifications, it will serve your purpose when baby is small and grow with him to suit future storage needs.

An upholstered wing chair for feeding, rocking, and cooing adds a lovely formal touch to a traditional nursery. Team it with a matching or coordinating ottoman if the room is spacious enough to accommodate one.

THE MULTIPURPOSE CHANGING TABLE

Diaper time can be learning time. When your baby is on the changing table, talk to him to introduce new words into his vocabulary. Gently touch parts of his body and say their names. This works especially well if you have a baby who hates to be changed, because it provides a great distraction from simply lying on his back waiting for you to finish cleaning him up.

---

gDIAPERS—GOOD FOR BABY, GOOD FOR THE PLANET

Breathable, flushable, incomparable! gDiapers are the latest wave of earth-friendly solutions for baby. They're made of an outer cotton pant that's washable and a nonplastic refill that can be flushed away. If you prefer, you can use the liners as compost and they'll break down in 50 to 150 days.

This is good news for the planet. According to the Real Diaper Association, an advocacy group founded in 2004, 27.4 billion disposable diapers are used in this country each year. The EPA translates that statistic into one of its own, stating that those numbers represent more than 3.4 million tons of waste dumped into landfills. Manufacturing disposable diapers also consumes huge amounts of petroleum, chlorine, wood pulp, and water.

WINDOW TREATMENTS

Drapes are an excellent choice in a traditional nursery. Fabrics might include toile or stripes, which make a brilliant statement on their own. If you prefer a solid, spice it up a bit by adding your own custom accent border. To lend a personal touch to store-bought window coverings, add a few inches of decorative fabric to the bottom.

For extra dimension, hang the drapes over Roman shades or wood blinds. For a Caribbean touch, try rattan blinds. If you prefer not to go with a multilayered window treatment, Roman shades and wood or rattan blinds work equally well solo.

Bold, strong hardware is beautiful and dramatic in a traditional nursery, so consider using substantial wrought-iron drapery rods with decorative finials. Metal pineapples and clear crystal finials are among my favorites.

BE WARY OF WALLPAPER

Much wallpaper is actually made of vinyl, which can give off dangerous chemicals. Vinyl also releases dioxin when it is manufactured, and according to the EPA, there is some concern that exposure to low levels of dioxins over long periods—or high-level exposures at sensitive times—might result in reproductive or developmental effects. If you have your heart set on wallpaper, look for a natural version. They're expensive, of course, but when you factor in safety, the price is worth it.

Also keep in mind that wall-covering adhesives are particularly chemical laden, so be sure to use an environmentally friendly, low-VOC version to go with your environmentally friendly wallpaper.

SAY NO TO FAUX

Window coverings should not be made of synthetic materials, since heat and light coming in through the window can cause synthetics to release gases into the room.

FLOORING

The floor is one of baby's primary environments, so this is one area of the nursery that should receive significant focus. It's important to use only natural fibers, such as wool, cotton, and silk.

I'm a big fan of area rugs on hardwood floors in a traditional room. I also like the idea of a rug that can grow with your child, and a company called FLOR makes that kind of versatility easy to accomplish. FLOR makes modular carpet tiles that mix and match. You can go with a solid color, a two-tone mix, or several different coordinating colors. You can even opt for a pattern, such as a floral or botanical.

Choose a predesigned rug in the size of your choice or create one of your own. Opt to cover part of the floor or extend the rug wall to wall. The tiles are available in different thicknesses—the extra plush one is best for the nursery—and no carpet pad is necessary. FLOR can be installed over any hard, flat surface, but don't use it over unsealed concrete or over an existing pad or carpet. Adhesive tabs keep the rug in place, so there's no slipping or sliding.

ROLL OUT THE SAFE CARPET

Synthetic carpets release toxic chemicals over time, so they should be avoided. Natural fibers, although more expensive, are safer choices. In addition, plant-fiber carpets made of sisal, sea grass, or jute are affordable, durable, and easy to clean.

BEDDING

As with all design styles, the bedding of your traditional nursery can be the jumping-off point for the entire look of the room. Shop for classic fabrics such as chenille and cotton, and consider buying fabric and having the bedding custom made. Stripes, paisleys, polka dots, and embroidery look fabulous in a traditional nursery, and are stunning when used together. As long as the color palette is the same, pattern mixing will work. If you have leftover fabric, use it to make a chair pillow or add trim to the cover of your changing pad.

The use of trim enhances traditional bedding, so go ahead and get frivolous with bows and frills if you have a little girl. A crib skirt is also a great way to help define a classic design style.

SWEET DREAMS

To reduce the risk of sudden infant death syndrome (SIDS), place baby on his back to sleep at least until he is a year old. Make sure he's on a flat, firm surface and that nothing else is in the crib. Guidelines established by the American Academy of Pediatrics recommend dressing your baby in footed sleepwear and eliminating the use of a blanket. If a blanket is used, it should be tucked under the mattress on both sides and on the bottom to prevent it from covering baby's face.

The U.S. Consumer Product Safety Commission (CPSC), the government agency responsible for protecting us from unreasonable risks of injury associated with products used in or around the home, has set the following requirements for children's sleepwear:

Infant sizes up to nine months—Sleepwear may be made from either flame-resistant or non-flame-resistant fabrics, because infants aren't mobile enough to expose themselves to sources of fire.

Infants sizes above nine months to children's size fourteen—Sleepwear must be made from either flame-resistant fabric or worn snug-fitting.

Flame-resistant sleepwear does not ignite easily and must self-extinguish quickly to meet CPSC flammability requirements. Flame-resistant garments may be worn either loosely or snugly. Although many flame-resistant fabrics are made of polyester, cotton can be treated to meet CPSC guidelines for flame resistance. Snug-fitting sleepwear, even if it is not fire resistant, is less likely to ignite and will not burn as quickly because less air is present between the fabric and baby's skin.

Never let your baby or toddler sleep in oversized garments such as adult T-shirts or sweatshirts, because they can catch fire more easily.

LIGHTING

Wall sconces—try mirrored ones—are a great way to light up a traditional nursery, and you can hook them up to a dimmer switch for maximum flexibility. In fact, I've used dimmer switches in all the nurseries I've recently designed. In addition to saving energy, they allow you to peek in on your baby at any hour of the day or night without waking him with a bright light.

Table lamps offer a diversity of options in a traditional nursery. Choose styles that can grow with your baby, such as art glass or a classic base with a tulip shade. You can cover the shade with your own fabric, or have the lighting store do it for you. To make it even more special, trim the shade with beads, fringe, or ribbon.

Additional options that reinforce the traditional style include hurricane table lamps, copper lanterns, and mica lampshades. The latter works particularly well if your design inspiration has its origins in the Arts and Crafts period.

WHAT'S BEEN BREWING IN *MY* BED?

When shopping for a crib mattress, keep in mind that most conventional ones are made from polyurethane foam, nylon, polyester, and vinyl—all of which are derived from petroleum. What's more, they're treated with chemicals in an attempt to safeguard against microbes, fire, stains, and wetness. A better choice is a mattress made from organic cotton, wool padding, and natural rubber.

Although appealing because they don't have to be ironed, permanent-press sheets are treated with formaldehyde, a known carcinogenic, making them a definite no-no for baby's room.

If you have trouble finding a crib bumper in a natural fiber, don't worry. Just be sure to wash the bumper in cold water before attaching it to the crib. It's more important for baby's sheet to be organic, because that's the fabric that will be coming into regular contact with his skin.

WARM, WELCOMING, AND SAFE

The nonprofit Home Safety Council of Washington, DC, has compiled these nursery safety guidelines—an invaluable checklist for parents. It is reprinted here courtesy of the organization.

The nursery should be a warm and safe environment where a baby can learn and grow. An active baby naturally climbs and crawls, rolls and rummages —and parents need to take precautions to make sure curious children avoid common home injuries. Consider the following tips to ensure that your child's haven remains safe and welcoming:

• Young children need close supervision, even in the nursery.

• To eliminate the risk of suffocation, remove all plastic bags from the nurs- ery area. If you want to protect special clothing, use cotton garment bags instead.

• Keep baby monitors and cords a safe distance from the crib.

• Store diaper products and medicines up high and purchase products with child-resistant packaging.

• Never leave the baby unattended on the changing table, and always use harness straps to secure the baby. Little ones learn in an instant how to roll over, and can tumble off while you turn away even for a second.

• Purchase UL-listed nightlights and replacement bulbs.

• Use only safety nightlight styles that prevent children from pulling out the nightlight or gaining access to the bulb. Use the recommended watt- age for the bulb and keep nightlights at least three feet from bedding and other combustible materials.

• Repair or replace frayed cords or damaged lamps. Be sure to hide cords behind furniture.

• Blind cords can present a serious strangulation hazard for early walkers. If your blind cords have continuous loops, call 800-444-6742 to request free repair kits.

• Install window guards with a quick- release mechanism that can be opened easily by an adult in case of fire.

• Keep cribs, beds, chairs, and other furniture away from windows.

• Anchor unstable furniture, including dressers and bookcases, to prevent them from toppling over.

• Install a baby gate at the nursery door.

• Choose toy chests with lid supports to prevent heavy lids from falling on children's fingers and necks.

• Use only one-piece rubber door- stops. Standard metal doorstops have small rubber caps that can easily be removed by little hands. These end caps are the number-one choking hazard in the home.

• Install finger pinch guards on doors or drape a towel over the hinge side to prevent painful pinching injuries.

special touches

A traditional style comes to life with family heirlooms, black-and-white family photos, shadow boxes filled with keepsakes, and favorite children's books. A French memo board lets you rotate items of interest for a new look every few months. A growth chart—a variation of the one you had as a child—adds true tradition to a classic nursery.

Create a unique entrance to the nursery with a Dutch door, which can double as a baby gate when the top half is open and the bottom half is closed. Adorn any door with a traditional metal doorknocker, and/or hang something fun and whimsical on the doorknob: a pair of baby booties, a brass key on a chain, an heirloom necklace.

A swing is a wonderful touch, affording both fun for baby and the added benefit of improving balance and strengthening the body's core. When doing research for *Feathering the Nest*, I came across some information on a product called the Cuddle Swing, which I think is pretty cool. It increases spatial awareness and promotes calming, and is often used for children with sensory integration issues. And here's the most fascinating part: when babies are delivered by Caesarean section, they miss out on the experience of progressing through the birth canal. As a result, they are sensory-seekers, and the swing fulfills that need.

In keeping with the Mother Nature feel of a traditional nursery, hang a hummingbird feeder or a birdhouse outside baby's window. Install a birdbath. If you're lucky enough to have a view of a tree that changes with the season—perfect. If not, plant a flowering shrub. Think of all of these as extensions of the nursery itself.

TUMMY TIME

Your baby's first few months are all about building movement; from holding up her head to rolling over; from sitting up to crawling. According to the American Academy of Pediatrics, regular time on her tummy will enhance motor development and help her meet these movement milestones.

Visual stimulation is another important component of tummy time. When lying on her back, your little one sees the ceiling and whatever happens to be directly on either side of her. When belly down, she can view more of her world from a more accurate vantage point.

To provide some encouragement, create a clean floor area in the nursery for tummy time—or clear a space where you can set down an organic blanket. Place baby on her tummy, sit or lie down beside her, and let her explore. And remember—tummy time is for waking hours, not when baby is asleep.

storage

Keep the traditional look going with a timeless toy chest—new or vintage, painted or stenciled. Shop around for large wicker baskets, and line them with fabric you've used elsewhere in the room. Look for old or reproduction hatboxes with lids. Both solutions make toys and playthings easily accessible and a snap to clean up.

For larger items, you simply can't beat an armoire. If your nursery can accommodate a large one, you're home free. If space is limited, many furniture manufacturers make scaled-down versions that still serve a very useful purpose.

If you decide on a nature theme, tree-trunk storage truly brings it home. Made of wood and designed to look just like the trunk of a tree, it's a straight-from-the-forest solution for stashing toys and playthings.

Wall-mounted shelves and freestanding bookshelves are ideal for displaying blocks and other wooden toys.

NICE TO MEET YOU!

Hang a nonbreakable metal or plastic infant mirror in the crib, playpen, or on a low spot on the wall, so baby can interact with a "new friend" and start building social skills. He'll be enchanted when he discovers that he can make his buddy touch his nose or wave his arms.

A mirror also affords a peaceful distraction when hung near the changing table. I've found it to be invaluable at diaper time, when Felix often tries out his dance routines while on his back. Mine is attached with an earthquake anchor for added safety.

GULP—AND IT'S GONE!

Make sure all choking hazards are out of reach. If it's small and looks appealing, it will likely head straight into baby's mouth!

PUTTING IT ALL TOGETHER
dottie's traditional nursery

Of all the nurseries featured in these pages, Dottie's is by far the largest, measuring twelve feet by fifteen feet. A recessed alcove with slightly lower ceilings and gloriously large windows sits at one end of the room, creating the perfect spot for a play area. This space adds another seven feet by ten feet to the overall square footage.

The inspiration piece for Dottie's nursery was the enchanting bedding by Serena and Lily in a design called Wren.

COLOR PALETTE

The main part of the nursery is painted a pale sage, while the play area is a soft butter yellow. Serena and Lily manufactures the paint, and the colors are called "sprout" and "sunshine," respectively. These paints are among the safest and least toxic on the market, boasting low VOCs and minimal odor. The doors, chair rail, wide baseboards, window frames, and all molding are painted bright white.

The colors are accented by touches of orange and darker shades of blue and green. A magnificent tree, complete with bluebirds, has been hand-painted on the walls—beginning in the play area, extending to the ceiling of the alcove, and branching out into the nursery. It's styled just like the crewel work on the Serena and Lily bedding—notice how some of the birds on the bedding and the birds in the mural are identical in design and color.

FURNITURE

Dottie's traditional sleigh crib is from PoshTots.com. Blending simplicity with elegance, it features smooth, graceful lines to lend a touch of sophistication. The crib is made of solid pine with a dark cherry finish. Features include a single drop side rail, hidden hardware, and three adjustable mattress levels to accommodate your growing baby. A crib drawer offers additional storage, and an optional conversion rail kit swiftly and easily turns it into a toddler bed.

The changing table, which I believe was originally from Pottery Barn Kids, was purchased from a secondhand shop. The finish is very close to that of the crib, so the pieces work well together. I added a new organic changing pad and found some baskets at a secondhand store and painted them white, which contrasts nicely with the dark wood. Baskets can be very expensive, so it's worth checking a local thrift store, flea market, or yard sale. Look for ones that are intact (no loose pieces) that might benefit from a coat of paint to regain their original sparkle. As an added touch, you can have coordinating liners made.

Both the antique daybed and the upholstered chair were finds at a used-furniture shop. I hope you'll bear with me while I digress just a bit and say that this store is one of those places where, at first glance, everything looks like it was abandoned in its greatest hour of need. Wood is scratched, scuffed, or scarred; upholstery is stained, faded, or torn; springs have sprung; and a pall of sad neglect—accompanied by a considerable amount of dust—hangs in the air. But oh, the hidden jewels that can be found there!

The key is to ignore the furniture's existing state of disrepair and learn to look for well-constructed woodworking and attractive lines. If the basic shape of the piece appeals to you, a bit of tender loving care can breathe new life into it. Solid wood can be stripped and refinished or painted. Upholstered items such as chairs and ottomans can be re-covered. And yet another shabby throwaway is plucked from furniture purgatory!

Of course, it takes a lot of imagination to envision what appears to be a piece of junk magically transformed into something beautiful. But over time, you'll find that you can add this skill to your repertoire. And from a planet-conscious perspective, it's this kind of reuse that makes us responsible stewards of the earth.

For the chair, I replaced the original damaged cushion with a down one, found lattice-work fabric in pale blue and sage green, and had the entire piece re-covered by a local upholsterer. The wood parts of the chair were painted white to match the trim in the nursery. The difference between the before and after is nothing short of pure drama.

As for the daybed, I could swear I heard it calling out to me as I wandered down the faded aisles of the store. It was collapsed in a sorry metallic heap when I first laid eyes on it, but I instantly fell in love with the intricate metal scrollwork. In spite of the fact that it was more antique than traditional in design, it was clearly a must-have for Dottie's nursery. When I brought it to the house and opened it up, it unfolded to reveal an absolute treasure of beauty and craftsmanship.

Because the daybed was sold only as a frame, I had a tufted cushion/mattress and two bolster pillows made for it by the same upholsterer who redid the chair. These are covered in white cotton with robin's-egg blue dupioni silk sides. Because of the light colors—beautiful, but not the most practical—I had the fabric treated for stain resistance. Both the cushion and the pillows feature apple-green dupioni silk piping—it's rather chunky on the bed and narrow on the bolsters.

Dottie's apple beanbag chair is by Easy Bean. Part of the company's Fresh Produce line, it's sized at thirty-one inches in diameter—tailor-made for children up to seven years of age. This fresh pick is handcrafted with detachable cotton velveteen leaves, and is available in the original 100-percent brushed cotton, like Dottie's, or customized in tech suede.

Eazy Bean is the brainchild of Francoise Sejourne, whose designs were inspired by several years of constant travel and the simple desire for a comfortable place to sit. From a mere thought, her concepts developed into more

than a decade's worth of work. The company's beautifully sculptured pods evoke feelings of humor, fun, and elegance through a unique use of color and timeless form. A global palette pulled straight from nature conjures up exotic images: the turquoise of Palau's waters, spice tones from the markets of New Delhi, lush pinks from the cherry blossoms of Japan.

With a focus on sustainable design and social awareness, Eazy Bean makes every effort to use environmentally sensitive materials and processes. For example, the company's tech suede is up to 100-percent post-consumer product, and the filling contains no chlorofluorocarbons (CFCs) and can be recycled. All products are made in the United States. From the beginning, Francoise has partnered with Goodwill Industries, a nonprofit organization, for fulfillment needs.

When Dottie is old enough to be the gracious hostess of a tea party, the perfect setting will be ready and waiting. The child-sized round table and two little stools, purchased used, is a charming place for her to entertain play dates, engage in an art project, or read a book with Mom or Dad. This is a great, inexpensive way to continue the nature theme, and the bright spring-green color is like bringing the park inside.

WINDOW TREATMENT

The traditional drapes were custom-made in blue and green dupioni silk, which is a medium-weight fabric woven with slubbed yarns. Its characteristics include a crisp, scrunchy hand; a beautiful luster; and an uneven texture.

FLOORING

Dottie's nursery has the original oak hardwood floors, which have been stained a deep cherry to match the crib and the changing table. The flooring in the play area was originally made of hexagonal terra cotta Mexican paving tiles—now covered with a faux-grass, moss-green modular rug by FLOR. Placed next to the little table and chairs, it adds to the Sunday-in-the-park feeling of the play area.

A strong sense of whimsy—and a delightful touch of nature—is inherent in the 100-percent wool, five-by-seven rug from PoshTots.com. It's called Dandelion Land, and the color palette combines all the colors used throughout the room. The rug has a soft, tufted texture that provides a lovely tactile experience. What better place for Dottie and her mom to spend some quality tummy time!

BEDDING

The unique beauty of the Serena and Lily bedding lies in the exquisite crewel work, done by hand on luxurious 350-thread-count Egyptian cotton. The bumper is embroidered on both sides with white ties and a zippered cover that removes easily for washing. The straight skirt is pale blue, with five box pleats and a white band with crewel embroidery. The fitted crib sheet is white Egyptian cotton with embroidered corners.

BREATHE EASY

According to the Environmental Protection Agency (EPA), the indoor air in a typical American home is three to five times more polluted than the outside air. To ensure that your baby's nursery and your entire home are as nontoxic as possible, look for products marked GREENGUARD INDOOR AIR QUALITY CERTIFIED. The Greenguard Environmental Institute (GEI) is an industry-independent, nonprofit organization that oversees the certification program by establishing acceptable air standards for indoor products, environments, and buildings.

GEI's mission is to improve public health and quality of life through programs that improve indoor air. The organization has established performance-based standards to define goods with low chemical and particle emissions for use indoors, primarily building materials, interior furnishings, furniture, cleaning and maintenance products, electronic equipment, and personal care products.

The GREENGUARD INDOOR AIR QUALITY CERTIFIED® mark is a registered certification mark used under license through the GREENGUARD Environmental Institute.

LIGHTING

Charn & Company's small acorn chandelier, which measures twenty-five inches in diameter, is clean, stylish, and fresh. Bands of dusty green accent the bright white finish, and the classic chandelier shades in green club stripe coordinate nicely with the Wren bedding. The table lamps I chose have a wooden base with a bright white finish. The medium-sized urn style is complemented by the flirty, flared shade in a matching green club stripe.

Charn & Company is a family business that has been around since 1995. Designer/owner Charn Pennewaert is committed to keeping traditional skills alive while creating designs that are elegant and refreshing. The company is recognized for its unique application method called panel designing, which allows printed fabrics—such as florals, checks, and stripes—to be transformed into lampshades of different shapes and sizes without distorting the direction of the pattern. Bouquets of florals are placed with intention, while checks and stripes match together in patterns that are pleasing to the eye.

Charn & Company also crafts an original line of hand-painted wood lamps. These custom creations are made from selected hardwoods and brush-painted to create a fine finish that complements a broad selection of custom fabric shades. The line includes an innovative ensemble of floor lamps, chandeliers, sconces, and table lamps — all handcrafted with attention to detail and design.

SPECIAL TOUCHES

The magnificent tree mural is the only special touch needed in Dottie's nursery. It makes such a spectacular statement on its own, and adding anything else to draw the eye would be a distraction.

STORAGE

The changing table provides excellent storage. Three drawers hold essentials such as diapers and baby wipes, and two deep shelves afford additional space for blankets and baskets filled with toys. Bookshelves at the base of the tree mural are the perfect catch-all for reading matter and toys.

VARIATIONS

The design of Dottie's nursery—from the color palette to the furniture to the accessories—is completely gender-neutral, so it suits either a girl or a boy. If you feel that the dandelions on the rug make it too girly, Serena and Lily makes a geometric color-blocked rug in the same palette called Poppy Square.

YOUR BABY *WANTS* TO LEARN

Visual stimulation in your baby's environment triggers curiosity and concentration, which is what every parent wants. But did you know that your baby wants it, too? Infants have an innate desire and a biological need to learn. The more stimulation you provide, the more circuitry is laid down for future learning.

"The human brain is unique in that it is the only container of which it can be said that the more you put into it, the more it will hold."

Glenn Doman, pioneer in the field of child brain development

adorable, affordable, art

PIQUING BABY'S CURIOSITY AND CONTINUING TO FIRE HER IMAGINATION AS SHE GROWS ARE VITAL TO HER DEVELOPMENT. THIS SIMPLE PROJECT HAS THE BENEFIT OF COMPLETE FLEXIBILITY, BECAUSE YOU CAN CHANGE IT AS OFTEN AS YOU WISH TO KEEP PACE WITH YOUR LITTLE ONE'S GROWTH AND INTERESTS. PERHAPS BEST OF ALL, THE COSTS INVOLVED ARE MINIMAL, GIVEN THE END RESULT.

MATERIALS YOU'LL NEED:

- A calendar—any size, any type, from any year—featuring baby animals, flowers, scenes from nature, famous paintings by the masters, or anything else that strikes your fancy

- Scissors

- Matte board

- Matte knife if you're cutting the mattes yourself

- Lengths of metal or wooden frames, cut to size

- Glass, cut to size

- An allen wrench or any other tool needed to assemble the frame

NOTE: These last five items can be purchased at a frame store or craft shop.

STEP-BY-STEP DIRECTIONS:

1) Select your favorites from the illustrations or photos featured on the monthly pages of the calendar.

2) Cut out as many pages as you'd like to use.

3) Cut the mattes to your desired width and frame size, buy pre-cut mattes, or have the frame shop cut them for you.

4) Take the overall dimensions of each matted piece, and have the frame shop cut the four pieces of frame and the glass to your specifications.

5) Assemble the frame pieces around the glass by fastening them with an allen wrench.

6) Presto! Your very own art gallery.

The framed calendar page featured here is the work of Jerianne Van Dijk, an artist from the Sierra foothills in California. Jerianne began her career as a graphic artist in a button factory, and, in her words, refined her talents in the prestigious school of "figure it out or die."

After several years with advertising agencies, newspapers, and freelance work for several printing establishments, she realized that her true joy in art is to create pictures—whether fine art, whimsy, or illustration.

Jerianne's artwork can be found in children's books and calendars, and it is available as original art and in limited-edition prints. If you prefer something in between, she also creates computer-generated drawing outlines (imagine a page from a highly sophisticated coloring book) that can be customized in watercolors in the palette of your choice.

When it comes to art for your baby's room, you can spend hundreds—or thousands—of dollars on an original piece, or you can simply get creative with a calendar. It's nice to know that even a budget-conscious parent can display beautiful artwork in the nursery for a song.

OPTIONS:

○ Matte and frame either one month's page from a large calendar or hang several smaller framed prints in a grouping.

○ Rotate the display again and again, using different calendar pages or photos from magazines or inexpensive books. Each new display can have a theme to keep things fresh and to spark baby's interest.

○ As your little one begins to create art projects of her own, use the mattes and frames for her priceless originals.

CHAPTER 4

international

"Have nothing in your houses which you do not know to be useful or believe to be beautiful."

—William Morris, English artist and writer

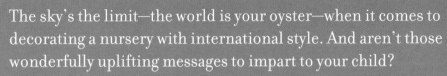

The sky's the limit—the world is your oyster—when it comes to decorating a nursery with international style. And aren't those wonderfully uplifting messages to impart to your child?

If you're a traveler, this is a great opportunity to bring your mementos into your little one's space. Those international experiences probably make up some of your fondest memories, so why not trigger them every time you walk into your baby's room?

Did you fall in love with the cathedrals of Tuscany when you spent a summer abroad living in youth hostels? Adorn baby's walls with sunlit photos of your favorite domes. Did you celebrate the honeymoon of a lifetime in Paris? Hang a framed map of *le metro* front and center so it's the first thing you see when you enter the nursery. Any visual that brings to mind a joyous memory for you should certainly be shared with your baby. If a particular destination or culture appeals to you, browse through books and magazines for ideas to spark your decorating imagination.

Even if your travels have been limited to books and movies, you still have every justification to add a global touch to the nursery. It can become your dream room, reflecting the places you'd like to visit with your child. Remember, just as an item can serve as inspiration for your decorating scheme, the room itself can serve as inspiration for future explorations.

A beachy feel works well in an international nursery, especially if you play up the exotic components of a tropical retreat. Bring in the natural elements that are indigenous to a particular culture by scattering seashells and pieces of coral across a dresser top. (Of course, they must become history as soon as baby is old enough to reach them and decide they'd make a tasty snack.)

Organic materials fit nicely into the casual, comfortable atmosphere of an international room. Choose cottons, linens, and poplins in florals, stripes, creams, and pastels. If you decide on upholstered pieces, consider washable slipcovers, which make cleaning them a snap.

color palettes

To impart a true international flavor, colors should make a statement with bold jewel tones or muted shades that resemble a watercolor. Pull hues from an inspiration piece that you might have found in a world market. Perhaps you've come across a colorful blanket from Guatemala. Decorate around the vibrant reds, oranges, and yellows. Maybe you want to display a collection of small, hand-painted Peruvian vases on a shelf. Play off their palettes of dusty sage, soft pumpkin, and smudged ochre.

Go for an international menu of food colors, like Jamaican mango and green papaya, Tahitian vanilla and Tuscan grape, French celeriac and Sicilian eggplant. Okay, so maybe I'm getting a little carried away with made-up color names, but I think you probably understand where I'm going. All of these combinations will work for a boy, girl, or surprise baby, and your inspiration just might come from the photos in your favorite ethnic cookbook.

If you opt to use a map as part of your wall décor, let it serve as the basis for your color scheme. Pick up aquatic blues from the ocean, deep greens from the forests, and misty purples from the mountains. A soft ivory is a beautiful base for these colors.

COLOR ME RELAXED...
COLOR ME STIMULATED

Color helps develop synapses, the critical chemical connections across the nerve cells of baby's brain. Soft blues, greens, and neutrals tend to be relaxing shades, while bright reds, oranges, and yellows are more stimulating. There's no advantage to one color over another, and the one you choose is a matter of personal preference.

guatemalan gold

slate blue

smudged ochre

jamaican mango

tuscan grape

dusty sage

tahitian vanilla

peruvian red

aquatic blue

Furniture

The furniture in an international-inspired nursery can be a wonderful mix of wooden inlay with beautiful upholstered pieces. Contemporary styles also work well because of the simple lines. I can't say this often enough: don't be afraid to mix things up. Quite simply, anything goes.

Moroccan styles that are low to the ground are very baby friendly. Reclaimed wood—whether light or dark—gives a rustic feel, and the imperfections add to its personality.

Bamboo furniture works beautifully in this type of setting, and can be found in cabinets, blanket chests, and side tables. As an aside to the reader: at the time of this writing, the bamboo furniture movement was relatively new. Not too many vendors carried a significant selection, but bamboo has all the earmarks of expanding in popularity. I sincerely believe that by the time *Feathering the Nest* is published, the availability of bamboo furniture—for a host of room applications—will be at your disposal.

NO DUMPING ALLOWED

When you're ready to dispose of a piece of furniture, think twice before putting it out with the garbage. Try selling it online, giving it away to a friend, or donating it to a charity. The last place it needs to end up is the landfill.

One man's trash is another man's treasure.

SCORE A COUP WITH BAMBOO

If you're looking for an eco-friendly furniture alternative, bamboo could be just what Mother Nature ordered. A quick-growing grass, it can sprout as much as two feet a day, depending on the particular species. Its extensive root system pushes forth new shoots whenever it's harvested, making it completely sustainable and renewable.

Bamboo has an attractive, delicate grain that's perfectly suited to furniture. It's also extremely durable, so it can take just about any abuse an active toddler can dish out.

One of the things I like best about bamboo is the fact that it enhances the environment. It helps prevent erosion by stabilizing the earth with its roots, it absorbs greenhouse gases, and it produces 35 percent more oxygen than an equivalent stand of trees.

window treatments

Play up the international flavor with rattan, bamboo, or wooden blinds. Or opt for Roman shades in sari fabric or trimmed in embroidery.

Coordinate your window coverings with the flooring. If you have dark hardwoods, balance and soften them with drapes flanking the windows. You can work wonders with gorgeous Asian silks. Or if you've had baby's bedding custom made, use the same fabric or a coordinating one on the windows.

MODULAR
CARPET TILES

As an alternative to wall-to-wall carpeting or an area rug, try easy-to-install modular carpet tiles. Made from renewable materials that are easily recycled, these squares are colored with nontoxic dyes and attached with low-tack adhesive dots. Removing and rearranging them is a snap, so you can change the pattern whenever you wish. And if your toddler spills juice on the floor, simply remove and wash the affected square and put it back or replace it with another tile.

When you tire of the carpet squares, simply send them back to the manufacturer for another round of recycling.

FLOOrING

Any type of hardwood floor will work well in an international nursery. If refinishing is required, be sure to do it long before baby is born, because sanding, staining, and sealing are messy and can be toxic. You don't want to undertake this task on your own when you're pregnant either, so hire someone who's used to doing this kind of work and knows what safeguards to employ.

Tile floors add punch to an international design, or—here it comes again—work with what you have. Regardless of what the floors are made of, be sure to create space for that all-important floor play by adding floor pillows, rugs made of faux hide, or timeless Asian rugs.

BEDDING

Your best bet is to find a bolt of fabric you love and have a few key pieces made, such as decorative pillows, a crib skirt and bumper, a baby quilt. If you are intent on an Asian-inspired room, you can find wonderful bedding in patterns of cherry blossoms or pandas. If you are having a hard time finding the right bedding, you can always start with a solid color and bring in patterns later.

Focus on organic cottons or hybrid organics, which often feature a blend of cotton and bamboo. These fabrics are surprisingly soft and feel as if they've been made just for baby.

If you're decorating for a little boy, patterned bedding with a nautical or aeronautic theme keeps the international concept going.

FOLLOW BABY'S LEAD

Some babies like things quiet; others respond better to noise and activity. Does she gurgle and babble softly to get your attention, or does she squeal and yelp enthusiastically? Her behavior reflects the kind of environment in which she's most content. Watch your little one for cues, so you can be sure to meet her needs with the types of toys she's most likely to enjoy. A naturally quiet baby will likely be more contented with a brightly colored picture book than with a fire truck complete with working siren.

If you offer her something and she turns away, squirms, or appears to distract herself in some other way, odds are she doesn't particularly like what you've presented. Follow her lead and move on to something different. Your baby will be happier and the bond between you will be stronger.

HOORAY FOR HEMP

Bedding made from weeds? You bet! Because hemp is a weed, it's grown without pesticides or herbicides, making it safe for baby and the environment. It's naturally anti-microbial, too, making it resistant to bacteria, fungi, mold, and mildew. Toss breathable, comfortable, and durable into the mix, and you have the perfect fiber for bed linens, diapers, and clothing.

LIGHTING

Incorporate unique lighting via stained-glass lamps or Moroccan or Japanese lanterns. Show your worldliness by using a lighted globe as a table lamp. Think outside the box—while you're at it, think outside the country—and look for light fixtures fashioned like airplanes or boats. Hang a chandelier for an elegant, old-world feel. Browse for wall sconces at a flea market.

BRIGHT IDEAS

- Choose a nightlight designed so the bulb cannot be touched.

- Keep nightlights at least three feet away from bedding, draperies, and other flammables. Better still, place them in the hallway outside the nursery.

- Do not use halogen bulbs in the nursery. They burn very hot and also pose a fire hazard.

- Place lamps on furniture that's in front of an electrical outlet, so both the cord and the outlet are out of baby's sight – and reach.

DON'T LET ARTWORK TAKE FLIGHT

When mounting artwork on the nursery wall, be sure to secure it with several nails or screws so it can't be knocked off. This is especially important in the area of the changing table, where baby's flailing limbs might send things flying.

special touches

Add international charm and intrigue by displaying artwork such as calligraphy, photos, or maps. Buy shadow boxes of different sizes and use them to display souvenirs from your travels. As your baby gets older, you can share stories about where you purchased these items and what they mean to you. By the time he's verbal, these mementos will be familiar to him, so your tales of their origins will be especially meaningful.

Hang fun things from the ceiling—paper umbrellas from Thailand, origami cranes made from exquisite Japanese papers, a model hot-air balloon, seashells threaded on ribbon or string. Antiques add the eclectic look that typifies international design, so look for old toys and hammered-metal vases from around the world. If you happen upon scraps of old silk, you can frame random pieces to create highly personalized and original artwork. Because a diversity of textures enhances this style, you might want to cover the walls—or one or two—with natural rattan.

Travel images conjure up an international feeling, so suspend a brightly painted toy biplane from the ceiling; display a sailboat, ship, or train on the dresser. These symbols of transportation can be incorporated into a mobile and wall art, as well.

NOT YOUR ORDINARY PAINT

To add a unique touch to baby's nursery that will grow with him through the years, consider magnetic or chalkboard paint. Magnetic paint is an acrylic latex water-based primer that transforms any wall into a surface that is receptive to magnets. Available as a dark gray primer, it can be covered with a top coat of latex or enamel paint in any color. Best of all, it does not contain lead and conforms to environmental VOC regulations.

Try magnetizing a portion of one wall, using narrow strips of wood to frame out the area. Just be sure to use large, sheet-type magnets so they are not a choking hazard, and attach them well beyond baby's reach.

Chalkboard paint turns any ordinary wall or closet door into a scribble palace. A low-VOC product, it creates a great blank canvas to encourage your budding Picasso.

For extra fun, combine the two. Apply three coats of magnetic paint topped with three coats of chalkboard paint to get the best of both worlds.

storage

Baskets or wooden boxes are a great storage solution. For a truly original look, find an old trunk and embellish it with travel decals from around the world. And once again, an armoire fits the bill perfectly in an international nursery.

Give new life to a standing wooden bookcase with several coats of paint. Start by applying a coat or two of a light color, then top it with a few coats of a dark color. Be sure to let each coat dry thoroughly before adding the next. When the paint is completely dry, use 60-grade sandpaper to rough up the edges of the bookcase, revealing the lighter color underneath. Don't be too heavy-handed and take it down to bare wood. The idea here is simply to show both colors and play them off one another. Try red over turquoise, orange over pale blue, navy over yellow. Your nursery's color palette will determine the shades you choose.

FOLLOW YOUR NOSE

When decorating baby's nursery, the sniff test is the best test. If anything you've purchased for the room smells offensive or has a chemical odor—from carpeting to bedding to toys—return it and replace it.

LESS IS MORE

While you want to create an enriching visual landscape for your baby, it's equally important to keep her space clutter-free. If there's too much going on at one time, the resulting chaos can be overstimulating. Opt for both open and closed storage, which allows you to alternate the things that baby can see. In this way, you keep things fresh and intriguing while avoiding brain overload.

PUTTING IT ALL TOGETHER
ben's international nursery

The idea behind Ben's nursery was to create a worldly adventure—in a ten-foot by eleven-foot space. As amazing as it sounds, that's really an attainable goal. There are so many wonderful options available today that enable you to create just about any kind of environment for your baby—and you don't need a huge amount of square footage to make it work.

The inspiration piece for Ben's room was a blue crocheted airplane that inexplicably captured the hearts of his parents when they started shopping for their soon-to-arrive son. It's designed by Anne-Claire Petit, who is from the Netherlands, and it's handmade in China by farmers who knit to supplement their incomes. Made of cotton, the airplane measures about eight inches long by eight inches high. What appeals to me the most is the fact that it's one of those delightful fabric toys that can be used as a design element or clutched lovingly in baby's arms.

COLOR PALETTE

Working with the blue of the little plane, I chose wallpaper in a blue, white, and gray hexagon design. It's custom made by Astek Wallcoverings, and was applied with nontoxic paste. To complement the blue, I added pieces of furniture in deep red.

THE PARIETAL LOBE

I'm not an expert on the brain, so I'll tread gently here. The parietal lobe is the area of the brain associated with touch, movement, recognition, and visual perception. It's also the place where artistic and musical appreciation take flight. Offering baby an assortment of toys and textures that he can explore stimulates the parietal lobe, helping him recognize objects, understand what he sees, and develop hand-eye coordination.

FURNITURE

Ben's crib and combination dresser/changing table are by PoshTots.com. The spindle crib, made of hardwood pine, is hand-painted in an antique brass finish and then hand-distressed to make it look as if it's been in the family for generations. (In keeping with my belief that it's okay to mix and match design styles, I've thrown in a piece of furniture that says "vintage," not "international"—and it works just fine.) The crib's features include double drop sides, rolling swivel casters, five mattress positions, and posture-perfect mattress support.

The mattress is organic—offering natural, firm support while reducing the risk of flattening soft bones in the skull and providing optimal weight distribution for an ideal balance of comfort and support. The organic cover is made of unbleached Pima sateen cotton and is removable for easy

care. I added PoshTots.com's optional mattress pad, which is covered in soft, organic cotton and filled with organic Cry Less Wool. The benefit of this fill is that it insulates against heat and cold and wicks away excess moisture before it has a chance to build up and disturb sleep. It also resists the accumulation of harmful allergens, helping to ensure Ben's health as well as his comfort.

The style of the dresser/changing table is called Cape Cod, and it offers extreme versatility. While it serves as a changer and drawer storage for Ben now, the top can be removed to convert it to a dresser when he's older. This three-drawer piece is handcrafted from solid wood, and it's available in dozens of hand-painted colors. I selected "hunting coat red" for Ben.

I found the spindle bookshelf in a secondhand furniture store, and gave it a new look with a few coats of red non-VOC paint to match the dresser. It's just the right place to display Ben's books and toys.

The rocking chair in Ben's nursery is a great success story. It has been in his mom's family for several generations, and when it eventually landed in her son's room, it was sponge-painted in a sort of acid yellow and charcoal gray. To say that it was…um…*hideou*s is a gross understatement. To make matters worse, it also had as many coats of different colors and finishes as it had owners. Stripping it down to bare wood involved the removal of no less than four layers! It is now the pride of the family and the highlight of the nursery, exquisitely finished in a rich mahogany stain that works well with the red furniture in the room.

The side table that sits beside the rocking chair is a work of art in itself. A thrift-store find, it was painted a soft blue and then decoupaged with travel images to reflect the international theme. A map was used as the background, and postcards from various destinations were glued on top.

Ben's antique red stool is from Morocco. Moroccan furniture is fantastic in a baby's room because much of it is designed lower to the ground.

THE CRADLE-TO-CRADLE CONCEPT

A popular phrase among environmentalists – coined by William McDonough and his firm MBDC—"cradle-to-cradle" refers to production techniques that are essentially free of waste. The idea behind the concept is that everything that comes out of the earth must be returned to the earth, meaning it must be put back into service by reusing or recycling, or it must be biodegradable.

WINDOW TREATMENT

Ben's room has wide windows along two walls. An ornate window treatment would have called too much attention to them, posing the risk of making the room look smaller. To keep things feeling open and airy, I decided on white plantation shutters for a crisp and practical solution. The shutters allow Ben's mom to completely darken the room at nap time, so they're both attractive and functional.

BABYPROOFING AS YOUR FAMILY GROWS

When you're expecting your first baby, ensuring that your home is a safe place is a relatively simple task, especially given the wealth of available products on the market. There's no one but adults in your home, so instilling responsibility isn't a problem. But when baby number two or three comes along, you're faced with adding a toddler or small child to the chain of safety responsibility, and that can be a challenge. Following are suggestions for how to make the task a little easier:

• Actively involve your older child. Teach her the dangers of leaving toys and other items in places where a baby might reach them. As an added precaution, routinely inspect all toys for small pieces that could easily detach or break off, sharp edges that could scratch or cut, and joints that could pinch little fingers. If something looks like it might cause even the slightest risk, dispose of it.

• Make it clear to your older child that small objects can cause choking, so he should never offer such items to the baby. Remind him that you did the same for him when he was tiny, and that these are the ways you keep your entire family safe.

• Take a look at any equipment you plan to reuse—high chair, bed, baby gates, car seat, and the like. Test them to be sure they're in good working order, and replace them if they're not. New and improved products may be available, so compare the latest offerings to what you have on hand and update if necessary.

• An older child's toys can pose a danger to her younger siblings. Be sure to evaluate and keep unsafe toys away from babies and smaller children.

• Potty training your youngest can present its own potential hazards, such as an older child who forgets to put the toilet lid down or to close the bathroom door behind him. To minimize these risks, install a lid lock and make sure your bigger kid understands the importance of using it. Remember—your little explorer can drown in less than one-half inch of water.

• Rig an alarm or chime on exterior doors to alert you when they're opened. Older children going in and out might forget to close them all the way, leaving the potential for little crawlers and toddlers to wander out.

Information adapted from Crumb Crunchers Inc. Baby Proofing and Child Safety Consultants

FLOORING

The hardwood floors are stained a dark mahogany, much like Ben's rocking chair. I balanced the deep-toned wood by adding a Moroccan-style wool rug from selectrugs.com. It has a 100-percent cotton backing, making it completely eco-friendly. I layered it with a three-by-five area rug that I found at Shabby Chic in Santa Monica, California. This patchwork Kilim rug is made from recycled pieces of carpeting that have been sewn together for a one-of-a-kind floor-covering solution. The color palette has a slightly sun-bleached appearance, and it picks up the blues and dark reds used throughout the room.

I can't mention the Shabby Chic store without sharing some information about Rachel Ashwell, the designer who founded the brand in 1989. Rachel is a sort of role model for me, because her designs are all about the aesthetics of beauty, comfort, and function—all of which I consider enormously important in my own work.

Says Rachel, "As both a mother and the creator of Rachel Ashwell Shabby Chic, my thoughts about decorating are that a home can be truly lived in and still be lovely. I believe in cozy relaxed settings where kids are free to put their feet on the sofa and guests can place their cups on the coffee table without a care. For me, the secret to living well is to surround myself with beautiful things that are practical and deliciously comfortable.

"My designs are inspired by flea market finds and the appeal of sensible living."

BEDDING

The bumper pad on the crib is covered in fabric featuring a blue-on-blue ethnic pattern. I found the fabric at a local store, and used the services of a local seamstress to line the bumper pad with organic cotton and put it all together. If you're having a difficult time finding baby bedding that you like, go on a fabric adventure instead and have it made. Using this option gives you virtually endless choices.

Ben also has an organic velour ruffled blanket in blue by PoshTots.com. It's earth- and baby-friendly all wrapped up into one—made in soft-to-the-touch certified organic cotton velour and trimmed with a matching natural silk ruffle. Also made with Mom in mind, the blanket is machine washable and dryable.

LIGHTING

I came upon the sconces for Ben's room at a small lighting store in Los Angeles. I loved that they looked both vintage and nautical, because that made them ideal for an international, travel-inspired nursery. I had them installed on a dimmer switch to conserve energy and enable them to be used as nightlights.

SPECIAL TOUCHES

You'll notice that I've used white wainscoting on Ben's walls —a decorating option that would more commonly be found in a traditional room. Again, giving yourself the freedom to pull elements from different design styles is what makes your baby's nursery utterly unique. The top of the wainscoting creates a narrow ledge, providing a convenient location for the TRAVEL sign over Ben's crib and a reproduction of an old poster that reads "Learn to Fly."

We've all heard about—and maybe even experienced— the young Jackson Pollock in training who takes a crayon to the living-room wall. With any luck, Ben's parents won't have to worry about using lots of elbow grease to remove their son's artwork, because the sliding doors on his nursery closet have been painted with chalkboard paint. When he's old enough for his creativity to take flight, his mom simply needs to keep a package of colored chalk on hand and set Ben free in front of his spacious "canvas."

Combining a special touch with convenient storage for books and small toys, the "See the World" wall panel by Zid Zid ties in with Ben's internationally themed room. Recycled cotton and cardboard have been used to create this playful and functional five-pocket panel adorned with animal imagery and graphics. Environmentally friendly features include the use of vintage fabric and buttons and 100-percent natural and untreated materials. As with all of Zid Zid's products, the wall panel is crafted by hand and produced in Morocco under fair-wage conditions.

Zid Zid was founded in 2003 by Julie Klear and Moulay Essakalli, a married artist/designer couple, after they moved from Cambridge, Massachusetts, to Marrakech, Morocco. Julie has exhibited her art in several American museums and has fifteen years' experience teaching art to children. Moulay, a graphic designer trained at the Rhode Island School of Design, was born and raised in Morocco and attended college in both France and the United States.

The couple believes that a child should have a good sense of both the world inside him and the world around him. As a parent, it is your role to foster your little one's imagination and help him learn about other places and other people. Zid Zid endeavors to help with this ongoing process.

All of the company's products reflect themes from nature and the animal kingdom. These are reproduced in intense colors to serve as exotic inspiration for your child. Combining a striking artistic sensibility with the colors and visual inspiration of Marrakech, Zid Zid's offerings blend the founders' creativity with the handiwork of Moroccan artisans, bringing the inner and outer worlds together for your child.

Ben's visual journey moves from Morocco to Japan as your eye travels around his room. Hanging over the changing table is a trio of paper cranes made by a young artist from Northern California. Just thirteen, Soleil Normand Smith loves all forms of art. She's a serious dancer, and takes classes in jazz, ballet, and hip-hop. She's also involved in a nonprofit organization called Haute Trash, designing outfits out of things like yogurt lids, candy wrappers, frozen-fruit bags, and even tape from cassettes and videos.

Her love of all things artistic has led her to master the art of origami, stringing her meticulously folded birds onto delicate threads and holding them in place with earring backs. She uses high-quality, heavyweight paper imported from Japan, which is widely available in a diversity of colors and patterns. In Ben's room, the cranes fly in front of a vintage map of the world.

Getting to know the parents—and getting them involved in the decorating process—is a big part of my approach to design. After all, they don't want to feel as if their baby's room is being designed by a stranger. Ben's mom and dad jumped right in when I asked them to gather an assortment of old family photos, including shots of themselves as children, which I framed and hung in a cluster on the wall. These charming, sentimental photos have a lovely nostalgic appeal that seems to fit right in with the eclectic nature of the room. A photo of baby Ben and his mom sits proudly in a dresser-top frame made from recycled wood and nontoxic paint and bearing the words "Mommy & me."

Odds are, Ben will go through a phase of wanting to grow up to be an airline pilot at some point during his childhood—he really has no choice, because his nursery is filled with flying machines. I've hung a mobile over his crib that features a globe and airplanes in orbit from House by Annette Tatum.

HEY...I HEARD THAT!

At birth, an infant's senses of hearing and touch are almost completely developed. With this in mind, it's a good idea to offer playthings that provide auditory and tactile stimulation.

Musical toys and mobiles will appeal to little ears. And don't forget reading and singing to your baby – the best aural stimulation there is.

Plush toys in a variety of textures will encourage exploration of little fingers and hands. Bear in mind that babies have usually mastered the three-finger pick up at six months of age, and have the pincer grasp down by twelve months.

STORAGE

Ben's closet was amped up for storage with the addition of a few basic components. In addition to the original rod and quilted hanging cubbies, it now features an assortment of shelves and drawers to store all his clothes and footwear. (And Ben has the most adorable selection of shoes, sandals, and boots I've ever seen!)

Several years ago, Ben's parents found a pair of spectacular antique red shutters in their travels to Singapore. The intricate Chinese engravings depict a children's story, so the couple stashed them away for the day when they could eventually use them in their baby's nursery. I opted to have a small cabinet made and to use the shutters as doors. The result is a magnificent work of art that also doubles as storage space.

VARIATIONS

Ben's nursery definitely has a little-boy feel to it, but it could easily be changed for a girl or a what's-it-gonna-be baby. The elements that make the room so boyish are the airplanes. I honestly don't know why means of transportation have come to be thought of as masculine, but that perception is firmly in place. If these components were eliminated and replaced with items that are specific to a particular destination, the room would appear more gender-neutral.

To alter it for a girl, think Paris. Do the wallpaper in rose, and change the airplane fabric of the bedding to a toile or a fleur-de-lis pattern. Add pink-and-black hatboxes for storage. Trade the Moroccan furniture for a small bistro table and chair with a padded seat—her very own Parisian café. Hang a French memo board on the wall. Or take the room to Tokyo, using cherry-blossom wallpaper and paper umbrellas. And remember—blue always works for a girl.

HEALTH AND SAFETY

The following tips are courtesy of Organic Grace in Garberville, California:

• Wash new nonorganic baby clothing and bedding—as well as the removable covers of car seats and swings—with a cup to a cup and a half of vinegar. This removes most of the toxic flame-retardant chemicals in many baby products. Use a drop of lavender essential oil in the wash to make it smell nice and to soothe baby.

• Use glass bottles to store breast milk or to feed your baby. Most plastic baby bottles use #7 plastic, which has been found to contain hormone disruptors. There have been no studies regarding long-term exposure to these chemicals, but a small one-time dose has been shown to disrupt brain patterns for hours. Polycarbonate plastic has also been linked to breast cancer.

• Avoid plastic teethers. Although many manufacturers have finally gotten rid of the toxic PVCs in their teethers, some have not. As an alternative, use organic cloth dolls and teethers, or wood teethers with nontoxic finishes.

Decoupage Side Table

YOUR MOTHER PROBABLY DID IT, SO DID YOUR GRANDMOTHER, AND HER MOTHER BEFORE HER. BUT DID YOU KNOW THAT DECOUPAGE DATES ALL THE WAY BACK TO 18TH-CENTURY VICTORIANS? DECOUPAGE IS THE ART OF ADORNING SURFACES—FROM BOXES TO FURNITURE TO TRUNKS TO TABLETOPS TO WALLS—WITH PAPER CUT FROM CARDS, WRAPPING PAPER, MAGAZINES, NEWSPAPERS, OR ANYTHING ELSE ON HAND. THE END RESULT CAN TELL A STORY OR SIMPLY PLEASE THE EYE—THE CHOICE IS YOURS.

Here's a fun and easy way to convert an ordinary side table into a worldly work of art, using a few basic tools and items straight out of your scrapbook, magazine rack, and travel memorabilia box. You can create a specific theme—Paris, Rome, Fiji, Bangkok, Africa, Mexico—or simply go for a general global feel. If you have a particular part of the world in mind, you might want to use a map of that region as a background piece. If you prefer something more universal, simply eliminate steps two through four in the directions that follow.

MATERIALS YOU'LL NEED:

- A side table from a thrift shop or discount store
- Map, postcards, plane tickets, train stubs, museum receipts, travel magazines, or any other paper items you'd like to add
- Scissors
- Precision knife, such as an X-acto
- White glue
- Water
- Small paintbrushes, either bristle or foam
- Craft brayer, a smoothing tool available at art supply stores; it looks like a cross between a mini paint roller and an equally teeny rolling pin
- Eco-friendly varnish

STEP-BY-STEP DIRECTIONS:

1) Make sure the surface of your tabletop is clean.

2) Cut out a section of the map to cover the entire surface of the table.

3) Apply glue to the tabletop and the back of the map, smoothing it out with the paintbrush. Carefully glue the map in place.

4) Eliminate any wrinkles or bubbles with the brayer or the flat of your hand.

5) Cut out images from your selection of postcards, photos from magazines, etc. using scissors or a precision knife. You can also add words cut from magazines, including the name of your specific destination, if applicable, or general words such as ADVENTURE, TRAVEL, EXPLORATION, EXCITEMENT, DISCOVERY.

6) Randomly arrange these images on top of the map—without using any glue yet—to determine the placement you like best. Add tickets stubs or any other souvenirs you might want to include from your travels. Loosen up a bit and try random angles and overlapping elements for a free-form look.

7) Take a digital photo so you'll know what goes where. If you're feeling particularly artistic, you can eliminate this step and simply go for it. You can't possibly make a mistake with placement, because randomness is all part of the decoupage process.

8) Remove the elements from the tabletop so the bottom layer can be glued on first.

9) Working in sections, apply glue to a small surface of the table, smoothing it out with the paintbrush.

10) Apply glue to the back of the cutout and position it in place on the glued area of the table.

11) Use the brayer on any wrinkles.

12) Continue in this fashion until all paper elements are in place, referring to your digital photo along the way.

13) After the glue has dried, apply three or more coats of varnish over the entire surface, allowing for drying time between coats. You'll know when to stop adding varnish when the edges of the cutouts are smooth.

CHAPTER 5

trace's tips

(oliver + felix's nursery)

"You are a marvel. You are unique. In all the years that have passed, there has never been another child like you. Your legs, your arms, your clever fingers, the way you move. You may become a Shakespeare, a Michelangelo, a Beethoven. You have the capacity for anything. Yes, you are a marvel."

Pablo Casals, Catalan cellist and conductor

My boys…my precious and amazing little boys. I sometimes wonder if I can ever look at them without feeling that familiar swelling in my chest that is nothing short of absolute awe.

Creating my children's nursery was pure joy. With each new component I added, I felt as if I was helping to shape their lives, stimulate their minds, give them the freedom to fantasize, invite them to laugh and have fun. Sometimes, when Oliver is playing in the nursery, I'll hear his voice ring out loud and clear: "Oliver's room! Oliver's room!" Knowing that he takes such sweet delight in his surroundings is an incredible gift to me.

Because the room was redecorated to accommodate the two boys, the inspiration piece became Oliver's big-boy bed. At the time of this writing he had recently turned three, and he had quickly transitioned from crib to toddler bed to full-size bed. (He's tall and lanky—one of those children who looks nearly twice his age—so the larger bed was a practical choice.) In addition to meeting his changing needs, it was important to include elements that would be appropriate for baby Felix, as well, and that became my most significant design challenge. The result is an eclectic mix that has a strong nature theme.

color palette

The walls of the nursery are painted a soft sky blue, and if you look very closely, you can see subtle white cloud patterns. The idea was to bring the outside inside, and that theme is maintained throughout the room.

When Barry and I first moved into this house and I was pregnant with Oliver, we planted a maple tree outside the baby's bedroom window. Artist Nancy Hadley painted a companion maple tree on the wzall of the nursery, complete with a frolicking brown squirrel and a bluebird. When we discovered that we had a resident peacock on the property, Nancy painted his likeness perched atop the bathroom door, his bright plumes trailing down the wall.

Because there's a considerable amount of furniture in this room, I kept the color palette relatively neutral to open up the space. Spots of bright color come from the wall murals and accessories.

"In choosing colors... follow nature's lead."
John Saladino, architectural and interior designer

red-orange

sky blue

maple

orange

bluebird

taupe

peach

fresh lime

oak

Furniture

The focal point of the room is Oliver's Dodu full-size bed. Made by Blu Dot, it's crafted of woven felt. A generously thick headboard with felt upholstery and French seams helps create a soft, sculptured, and low-profile look. The color I chose is a neutral called wheat.

The story behind Blu Dot is an engaging one. Three college friends – John Christakos, Charles Lazor, and Maurice Blanks—shared a passion for art, architecture, and design. After they finished school and began to furnish their first homes, they didn't like the things they could afford and they couldn't afford the things they liked. So they decided to do something about it. Blu Dot was born in 1997 with the goal of bringing good design to as many people as possible. The company is committed to creating products that are useful, affordable, and desirable.

Their offerings are also kid-friendly. Oliver loves to climb on the headboard and jump off onto the mattress. Because the entire bed is so soft and low to the ground, I don't immediately shift into mommy-worry mode when he engages in his impromptu gymnastics routine.

The mattress that gets so much of Oliver's attention is the Keetsa Cloud. The core is made with high-density memory foam, and every part of the mattress is composed of recyclable materials. EverGreen, made from all-natural green tea, is embedded into the foam for long-lasting odor control. Green tea is becoming increasingly recognized for its calming effect and powerful antioxidant capabilities, and Keetsa's unique use of the product effectively reduces the emissions of harmful VOCs and off-gassing in the foam. The cover is unbleached and breathable 100-percent cotton, with channel quilting for comfort and support.

Here's something about Keetsa mattresses that I find truly interesting. The company utilizes a patent-pending process that allows the mattresses to be compressed and shipped in surprisingly small packages. They bounce back into

their original shape when they're unpacked in your home, having left behind a much smaller carbon footprint than that of traditional mattress packaging. What's more, the compact size of the box reduces freight costs. This works for me, because I believe that every little bit helps when it comes to safeguarding our planet.

Opposite Oliver's bed is Felix's crib, designed and manufactured by Oeuf and available from 2Modern. Although the sides are fixed, the adjustable mattress height and low profile make it easy to reach into. The sides, headboard, and footboard are all cut from single panels of wood to eliminate the risk of loosening joints. The side rails, finished in white lacquer, are environmentally friendly medium-density fiberboard (MDF) made from recovered wood fibers. The legs are metal and the base, which I selected in a walnut stain, is solid birch. A matching changing table—complete with pad—attaches to either end of the crib, offering a great space-saving convenience. The crib mattress is the organic one by PoshTots.com that I've used in most of the featured nurseries.

With an eye on the future, Oeuf offers an easy-to-use conversion kit for this crib. All you have to do is remove the side panels from the base and replace them with the toddler-bed side panels and *voila!*—a familiar and comfortable space to fit your growing child's growing needs.

Oeuf also makes the boys' Mini Library, which houses their books and a scattering of toys. In white lacquer and walnut to match Felix's crib, it's carefully designed to place the contents within easy reach of little hands.

Like the contours of its namesake, Oeuf (which means "egg" in French and is pronounced like the "uff" in stuff) is about simple, clean design applied to the necessities of a well-equipped nursery. Oeuf's founders and designers, Sophie Demenge and Michael Ryan, are a French-American husband-and-wife team based in Brooklyn, New York. The company was created when Sophie and Michael became first-time parents in 2002. As part of a new generation of design-conscious and environmentally aware parents, they realized they had to

THAT'S A WRAP!

Instead of tossing that pretty wrapping paper, run it through your shredder to make stuffing for gift bags. You can combine patterns that work together, make a special holiday batch, or just toss it all in together in a colorful bundle. The next time your little one goes to a birthday party, you've got a head start on the packaging.

redesign everything themselves to merge their existing esthetics with traditional nursery design. They believe strongly that while babies don't need many items, they do need some essential pieces. Oeuf's mission is to make those essentials practical and stylish without compromising quality and safety – their top priorities.

The side table next to Oliver's bed was reappropriated from elsewhere in the house. I encourage parents to use existing pieces of furniture whenever possible, because doing so saves money and saves the planet.

Beneath the tree on the wall sits a white Herman Miller - Eames molded plastic armchair with a rocker base. It was designed by Charles and Ray Eames, who adapted molding techniques developed during World War II to mass-produce this classic design. Always interested in new materials, they saw plastic as an opportunity to form organic seat shells that conform to the body's shape. The enduring forms and quality construction are rendered today with updated materials that are more environmentally friendly.

This chair was first presented at the Museum of Modern Art in 1948, and the 21st-century version in the boys' room looks precisely the same as the original. Clearly, great design has extraordinary staying power.

The desk beside Oliver's bed was made by a local artisan. I wanted my little project manager to have a place to work on his various creative tasks, but the space was too small for a standard desk. I gave the artisan the dimensions of the allotted spot, and he designed the desk to fit.

He also made the corkboard that hangs above it, which is used to display the artwork that Oliver creates in preschool. The desk chair was originally in our home office. Already bearing a few scuffs and scratches, it's well suited to all the additional wear and tear Oliver has been giving it. The light-up globe that sits on the desk is a vintage piece I found at a flea market.

WINDOW TREATMENT

The multicolored Roman shades that were over Oliver's bed before Felix was born were too visually overwhelming when the inevitability of growing up and the need for sharing space called for a bigger bed *and* a crib. I replaced them with white plantation shutters, which I also used on the small single and double windows that sit high on the side wall. They blend nicely with the pale blue and white paint on the walls, let in lots of light when they're opened, and darken the room considerably when closed. I especially like the fact that Oliver can open and shut them on his own—no dangerous cords to get in the way.

FLOORING

I opted for prefinished natural bamboo flooring that was purchased from Lumber Liquidators and manufactured by Eco-World Flooring Company. The light-colored finish reflects the true color, grain, and growth pattern of the bamboo while visually expanding the room. If you prefer darker flooring, choose the carbonized finish—a darker caramel shade throughout. Because of the natural grade of all bamboo flooring, it's likely to have some tonal variation, mineral coloring, and small pin knots, which I think add to its overall beauty.

BEDDING

Oliver's bedding is from modernnursery.com. Both quilts are made of 100-percent organic cotton, colored with dyes that are nontoxic and biodegradable. The Season pattern is embroidered onto a 50-inch by 60-inch throw that reverses from persimmon orange to lotus green with an edge of sable brown. The 30-inch by 40-inch Transport throw reverses from ozone blue to lotus green with the same sable edging. The sheets are made of a bamboo-cotton blend.

Felix's bedding is Embroidered Circles, an organic crib set by DwellStudio. Simple yet sophisticated, the pieces include a reversible bumper, fitted sheet, crib skirt, and blanket—all made of fine Portuguese cotton. The fabric is not chemically treated in any way, and no dyes or bleaching were used at any point in the production process.

LIGHTING

The primary light source comes from track lighting tucked surreptitiously into the multilevel beams of the ceiling. Tiny amber shades on the lights virtually disappear into the color of the wood, so all you really see are the chrome bars. A dimmer switch allows me to control the level of light with ease. More concentrated lighting comes from the lamp on the bedside table. I found a base I liked at a thrift shop, painted it yellow, and plunked on a shade from another lamp in the house that was ready for its own facelift.

Above the nursery door is a light-up moon that sets the mood for story time. Because it can be controlled by a remote switch, Barry and I can turn it off and tell Oliver the moon has gone to sleep when it's time for him to do the same. Works like a charm every time!

special touches

The animal kingdom shares the boys' room via several pillows on Oliver's bed and on the floor. Made by Amenity and part of the company's Meadow and Woods collection, they feature bunnies, birds, turtles, deer, and more in a refreshing palette of green, yellow, orange, and cocoa. The pillows measure twenty-six inches by twenty-six inches and are printed with eco-friendly, water-based dyes onto 100-percent hemp/organic cotton fabric. The backing is the same material done up in solid cocoa.

You can choose from two environmentally responsible insert options. Eco-fill is a high-quality polyester fiber generated from spun recycled bottles, and kapok is a natural, downy fiber from the seedpods of the kapok tree. Both fills are encased in an organic cotton shell.

storage

Most of the storage for the boys is hidden away in their adjacent walk-in closet. Hanging rods, a built-in dresser, and assorted shelves hold their clothes, shoes, and extra bed linens, and baskets on the floor of the closet are a tidy way to stash toys. Additional storage is provided by the tree-trunk bin that sits near the foot of Oliver's bed.

variations

Because I've decorated around elements of nature, Oliver and Felix's shared room is appropriate for boys, girls, or both. The blue walls could be painted pink to make it more feminine—or yellow for gender-neutral—but a change isn't really necessary.

MONSTER SPRAY

Oliver likes us to have monster spray on hand, just in case he and his baby brother need to be protected from the ghosties, ghoulies, and beasties that might dare to lurk in the sanctuary of their nursery. One spritz in the closet and under the bed and the monsters are history!

Several commercial varieties of monster spray are available, but you can make your own all-natural concoction by filling a spray bottle with water and adding a few drops of lavender oil. Other essential oils will work, as well, but it's a good idea to avoid anything that smells good enough to drink—such as vanilla or orange. And, of course, spraying the monsters should always be an adult-supervised job.

DECORATING FOR TWO...OR THREE...OR MORE!

If twins or more are on the way, you're faced with a whole new set of design challenges. Suddenly, you're thinking about accommodating multiples of everything – from cribs to dressers to essential accessories. And if you happen to be having babies of both genders, there's the added issue of finding a design solution that works for both boys and girls.

Odds are, you've made the decision to put your babies in the same nursery. It's only natural, given the fact that they've just spent nine months in pretty close quarters. Some parents believe that separate rooms will prevent the crying baby from disturbing the slumbering sibling, but my friends with multiples disagree. Their experience has been that twins and triplets are more content and sleep much better when they're close to their brothers and sisters. It makes sense to me. After all, imagine the shock of being alone in a strange new environment after such sociable womb time!

I know parents who've used a single crib for twins for the first few months, stating that it's soothing for the babies to be close to one another. I know others who refuse to co-bed their babies because they perceive an increased risk of SIDS. There's information out there to support both sides of the argument, so my suggestion is to talk to your pediatrician and follow his or her advice.

The general consensus is that twins should be in separate cribs—positioned so the babies can see one another —by about four months, so we'll start at that point. Let's

work on the assumption that you have two newborns who are sharing the same room and sleeping in separate cribs. (If you have more than two babies, you can easily modify the information that follows.)

The good news is that the crib is the only piece of furniture you really need to duplicate. Try placing them side by side, with the head of each crib against the wall. Paint a bright rectangle or square behind them, creating the illusion of a headboard for a unified look.

A single changing table and rocking chair will serve your purposes for at least the first few months. After that, you can regroup and decide if you need to make any additional changes.

My main advice when decorating for twins is to keep it simple. Clutter will become your enemy in a big hurry, so make sure your space is organized. "A place for everything and everything in its place" will become your new mantra—and the key to your sanity.

Storage and functionality are tops on the list when outfitting a nursery for more than one child, so look for a changing table with drawers and/or open shelves. This will enable you to place everything you need for diaper duty right at your fingertips. Keep diapers and baby wipes close at hand by putting them in open baskets on a shelf. Store changes of clothes and extra blankets in the drawers.

If the nursery is just too small for two—if you have visions of constantly bumping into walls and furniture in your attempt to care for your twins — you might want to think about sacrificing the master bedroom just for the first two or three years. Giving up your haven might be worth it if the extra space and storage room translates to making your life a little easier.

After I gave birth to both Oliver and Felix, my life was all about meeting their needs and simply making it from morning to night in one piece. I can't even begin to imagine what it must be like with multiple babies! Mommies of twins and more, I applaud you. Be kind to yourselves and maintain your focus on doing what you have to do to keep your babies happy and healthy. And look at it this way: we all have to teach our children to be kind and to share. You have the advantage of getting a head start!

organizing baby's closet and dresser

Odds are, you'll have clothing in a variety of sizes as soon as your baby arrives. In addition to dozens of newborn onesies, it's not unusual to receive gift outfits and hand-me-downs that range from six to twenty-four months or beyond. Instead of lumping everything together and then struggling to find the right size at the right time, divide clothing by size from the start and store accordingly.

For example, if you have a six-drawer dresser, devote the top two drawers to newborn items, the middle two to size three to six months, and the bottom two to six to nine months. Keep larger sizes on color-coded hangers in the closet, using one color for sizes nine to twelve months, another color for eighteen to twenty-four months, and so on. If you prefer not to hang clothes that you won't be using for a while, purchase plastic storage bins, label them by size, and store them in baby's closet. Then, as you receive additional gifts or gently worn items, you can put them in the right-sized container.

Since baby clothes don't require much hanging depth, consider raising the existing closet rod and adding another rod below it. You'll immediately double the amount of hanging space at very little cost. If you want to splurge on a closet organizer, you can have one custom made to meet your clothing storage needs.

maximizing space in a small room

Your baby is on the way, and you want to fill her room with every imaginable item that will meet both her needs and yours. The dilemma: your nursery measures eight feet by nine feet, and no matter how long and hard you stare at the space, it's not getting any bigger.

There's no need for magical intervention. No need to bring in a construction crew to knock out the walls. With a bit of careful planning and organizing, you can make the most of whatever space you have.

Small rooms can make a big impact, so instead of getting discouraged and feeling that you have limited possibilities, look at the glass as half full. Your baby really doesn't need masses of furniture, so establish some practical guidelines about what is truly essential. If there isn't space for something, you probably don't need it anyway.

Color Palettes – A neutral pastel shade on the walls is an effective solution, but it's not your only option in a small room. Contrary to common belief, dark colors do not necessarily make a room look smaller. In fact, you can create visual depth by painting two opposing walls a deep color, such as blue, violet, or green. These cool tones —the colors of the sea, sky, and forest —will appear to recede, making the room appear larger.

If you prefer, focus on a single wall, anchoring it with a bold paint treatment that contrasts with the other three. A colorful wall covering or wallpaper also serves as an ideal accent to expand the room.

Alternatively, choose a color that you like and apply it in a monochromatic scheme – varying shades of the same color. Or pick different colors that have the same tone and intensity, such as cobalt and purple. Both treatments will give you the opened-up feel you're looking for.

Furniture – The baby's bed will most likely be the largest piece of furniture in the nursery. I suggest using a crib with a streamlined design—something basic and no-fuss without a canopy or any ornate details. Clean lines allow the eye to travel freely about the room, making it feel more spacious. Because of its sleek and simple design, contemporary furniture works best when you're faced with limited square footage.

Before you set out to buy baby furniture, take a look around your house. You might already have a small side table or dresser that can be put to new use in the nursery. Once you've taken inventory and reappropriated what you can, it's time to hit the stores.

When shopping for a bookshelf or chest of drawers, look for pieces that are tall and narrow, since they take up less visual space than furniture that's short and wide. Ample space between items helps open up a room, as does keeping furniture away from doors.

Make sure the pieces you choose are relatively small and scaled down, and buy only what you absolutely need. Even though you might be enchanted by the vast storage possibilities of a bulky oak armoire, it will likely overwhelm the room. Instead, look for combination pieces that serve a dual purpose. Several manufacturers make double-duty furniture, such as a changing table that includes a chest of drawers; crib with built-in storage beneath; two-tiered toy box that serves as a step stool when baby gets bigger. If it takes up the space of one item but serves the functionality of two, it's a smart buy.

Window Treatments – Use minimalist window treatments to open up the room. Simple blinds or light-colored Roman shades with a tailored valance are a good choice. Try hanging the valance higher than the top of the window to make it appear taller and to elongate the entire room as a result.

Flooring – Basic is best. You don't want to draw attention to the floor in a small room, so avoid busy patterns and fussy designs. Instead, choose wall-to-wall carpeting in a neutral color and a light texture. Cork flooring is also a good choice, because it's soft enough not to require the addition of an area rug, which can break up a room and make it appear even smaller.

Bedding – Once again, keep it simple. Avoid noisy patterns and lots of embellishments. If the design is such that it screams for attention, it will overwhelm a small nursery. Blending the color of the bedding with the color of the walls is a good solution to open up the room.

Lighting – Use natural light to your advantage. You'll be amazed at how a sunny window can make a room seem larger than it really is. Inside the nursery, track lighting will eliminate the need for lamps, which take up visual space. Install a dimmer switch so you can control the brightness of the room.

Special Touches – Keep accessories to a minimum. There's no need to top every piece of furniture with masses of toys, stuffed animals, and chotchkes that serve no other purpose than to clutter up the room.

Mirrors are a wonderful multipurpose solution in a small nursery. Besides giving the illusion of more space, they reflect light and the great outdoors when placed opposite a window. They'll open up the entire room and bring in twice the natural light, making the nursery feel open and airy. Best of all, babies love to see their reflections.

Storage – This is the most crucial word when it comes to decorating a small space. You need all the storage you can get, because if items are out of sight, they can't cause visual overwhelm.

A crib skirt can provide a screen for a multitude of objects. Store less frequently used items beneath the crib —your extensive stash of diapers, for example—where they'll remain hidden by pretty fabric. It's also a great place to hide away plastic storage bins that can be filled with toys, blankets, or baby clothes that don't yet fit. Alternatively, look for a crib that has drawers beneath it or find a bench that doubles as a toy chest.

To expand floor space and open up the room, rethink baby's closet. Remove the door and treat it as an alcove for your changing table or dresser. Or take down the hanging rod and install floor-to-ceiling shelves.

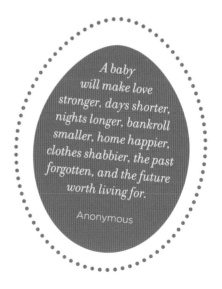

A baby will make love stronger, days shorter, nights longer, bankroll smaller, home happier, clothes shabbier, the past forgotten, and the future worth living for.

Anonymous

THINK COZY

There are definite advantages to a small nursery. When space is limited, you can't possibly become a pack rat, so consider this an opportunity to teach your baby an early lesson about the benefits of being streamlined and tidy. Working within the confines of limited square footage also affords a chance to kick your creativity into high gear, because you'll need to make every furniture choice count.

In truth, the size of the nursery is all about *your* perspective. Instead of thinking of it as tiny, appreciate it for its compactness, efficiency, and coziness. And if it's an environment where baby is comfy and happy, it's the perfect size and place.

A New Life For Baby Furniture

As any parent will attest, kids grow up fast—sometimes too fast. One day you're decorating the nursery in anticipation of your new arrival, and in what seems like no time at all, you're gearing up for kindergarten. (At that rate of speed, can the senior prom be far behind?)

As I've mentioned so many times in this book, responsible decorating is all about reusing and recycling items whenever possible. So when the time comes for you to give up that lovingly used piece of baby furniture, you have several options at your disposal.

The first and most obvious choice is to pass it on to someone who can make use of it: a family member, friend, neighbor, or charitable organization. If you prefer to hold on to it for sentimental or other reasons, you can put it to use in an innovative way.

Paint the entire surface of the table with enamel or high-gloss paint. It's a good idea to apply several coats, since greater coverage will help resist the effects of rain and snow. The shelves and drawers can be used to store potting supplies, and cup hooks attached to the sides of the table can be used to hang gardening tools. If mobility is important, attach small wheels to the bottom of each leg.

If your baby's toy chest is embellished with kiddy motifs, apply several coats of new paint or strip and sand it for a natural wood finish. Toss in a few cedar blocks and use it to store blankets or pillows. Place it at the foot of your bed or your older child's bed, and the warm cozies are right there when you need them. You can also convert it to a bench seat, adding a padded cushion to the top.

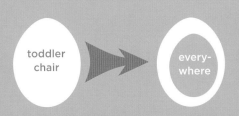

A little chair can be put to several different uses when your little one has graduated to a big-kid chair. Use it virtually anywhere in the house as the base of an art display. Place a framed photo, painting, decorative basket, or vase on the seat, and change the display whenever you tire of it. If the chair is small enough, another option is to hang it on the wall and use it as a decorative shelf. It can be painted to coordinate with a particular room, or stripped and stained to a neutral wood tone and rotated throughout the house.

Remove the dresser drawers and use them as open shelves to store DVDs and videos. If necessary, stain the piece or give it a fresh coat of paint.

When there's no longer a need to have a rocker in the nursery, move it to a home office, den, or living room.

THINK AHEAD

When shopping for baby furniture, consider tomorrow's needs, as well. Look for pieces that can outlive a nursery or toddler's room, such as an armoire, side table, daybed, or upholstered chair. These items will be highly useful when your child is small, and can also be given new life elsewhere in your home when baby outgrows them.

FINAL WORDS OF ADVICE

As you begin your decorating journey, hold on to this thought:

Truly good design endures. It never falls victim to trends; it doesn't limit itself to themes. It draws effectively from the past, flourishes brilliantly in the present, and transitions comfortably to the future. It is both fashionable and personal, gracefully and authentically reflecting the character and lifestyles of those who call it home.

vendors and resources

BABY SKIN CARE

Badger Balm
www.badgerbalm.com
organic baby skin care
(800) 603-6100

California Baby
www.californiababy.com
organic baby skin care
(877) 576-2825

BEDDING

Amenity Home
www.amenityhome.com
organic nursery bedding, stretched canvas
(213) 624-7309

Caden Lane
www.cadenlane.com
bedding, accessories
(210) 687-1919

DwellStudio
www.dwellshop.com
bedding
(212) 496-1394

House Inc.
www.houseinc.com
cottage style and striped bedding
(310) 449-1918

Keetsa Mattresses
www.keetsa.com
1.8.777.KEETSA (1-877-753-3872)

Victoria Mae
www.victoriamae.net
bedding and accessories

CLOTHING AND ACCESSORIES

Baby Bambu
www.babybambu.com
bamboo clothing and bedding
(201) 637-5244

Balboa Baby & Co., LLC
www.balboababy.com
Serene Sling baby sling
(949) 200-7541

Bla Bla Kids
www.blablakids.com
clothing and toys
(404) 875-6496

Isabooties
www.isabooties.com
eco-friendly baby shoes
(703) 380-6067

Kate Quinn Organics
www.katequinnorganics.com
clothing and custom quilts
(206) 778-4141

Tea Children's clothing
www.teacollection.com
(866) 374-8747

DIAPERS

gDiapers
www.gdiapers.com
eco-friendly baby diapers, colored with flushable inserts
(866) 553-5874

FLOORING

Angela Adams
www.angelaadams.com
rugs
(207) 774-3523

FLOR
www.flor.com
carpet squares made from the company's program that recycles old and returned carpeting
(866) 281-3567

Lumber Liquidators
www.lumberliquidators.com
hardwoods and cork flooring
(757) 566-7493

Select Rugs
www.selectrugs.com
assorted rugs

FURNITURE

Eazy Bean
www.eazybean.com
eco-friendly beanbags, floor pillows, cubes
(561) 620-0208

Jennifer Delonge
www.jenniferdelonge.com
eco-friendly and vintage furniture
(858) 349-5790

Monte Design (Canada)
www.montedesign.net
gliders, cubes, bassinets, and cribs
(866) 604-6755

Netto Collection
www.nettocollection.com
cubkids.com
modern baby furniture and accessories
(212) 343-1545

2Modern
www.2modern.com
modern furniture
(888) 240-5333

Joseph Wahl Arts and Joey Baby
www.josephwahlarts.com
(818) 340-9245

Herman Miller
www.hermanmiller.com
furniture and seating
(616) 654-3000

LIGHTING

Charn & Company
www.charnandcompany.com
(714) 318-8682

Maura Daniel Lighting
www.mauradaniel.com
(310) 838-8844

STROLLERS AND BASSINETS

Orbit Baby
www.orbitbaby.com
completely green and environmentally
   friendly strollers and bassinets; funders
   of sustainable-energy products
(310) 385-1124

SPECIALTY ITEMS

B Green
www.bgreenhangers.com
child-size bamboo hangers
(800) 452-1679

Bomar Designs
www.bomardesigns.com
composition ornaments
(913) 837-3202

Closets to Go online
www.closetstogo.com
(888) 312-7424

**Crumb Crunchers Inc. Baby Proofing and
Child Safety Consultants**
www.crumbcrunchersbabyproofing.com
in-home safety consultations, full line of
   child-safety products

Nancy Hadley
www.nancyhadley.com
art and design

Second Street Framing
www.secondstreetframing.com
(310) 440-8814

Jerianne VanDijk
www.jerianne.net
hand-painted murals, watercolors, illustrations
(530) 271-7128

TOYS AND ACCESSORIES

Bla Bla
www.blablakids.com
toys and clothing
(404) 875-6496

HaPe Toys
www.hapetoys.com
eco-friendly wooden and plush baby toys
(262) 227-8949

Petunia Pickle Bottom
www.petuniapicklebottom.com
diaper bags and organic cotton accessories
(310) 385-1124

Plan Toys
www.plantoys.com
eco-friendly wooden and plush baby toys
(650) 968-4783

Taraluna
www.taraluna.com
eco-friendly baby accessories
(877) 325-9129

Zid Zid
www.zidzid.com
organic toys

WALLCOVERINGS
AND PAINT

Astek Wallcoverings
www.astekwallcovering.com
wallpaper designed with custom patterns
  on recycled paper with vegetable ink
(818) 621-8511

The Old Fashioned Milk Paint Co., Inc.
www.milkpaint.com
paint made from a milk base

Serena and Lily
www.serenaandlily.com
non-VOC paint
(415) 331-4364

Talissa Décor
www.talissadecor.com
wall and ceiling tiles
(888) 717-8453

Thibaut Wallpaper
www.thibautdesign.com
wallpaper and fabric

WINDOW TREATMENTS

Select Blinds
www.selectblinds.com
all window treatments

THE WORKS

Baby Universe
www.babyuniverse.com
all baby products
(303) 226-8685

Dreamtime Baby
www.dreamtimebaby.com
all baby products
(303) 226-8685

Organic Grace
www.organicgrace.com
organic bedding and an extensive selection
  of organic and nontoxic items for the
  home, baby, and mom
(707) 923-1296

PoshTots.com
www.poshtots.com
all baby products
(804) 921-7660

Serena and Lily
www.serenaandlily.com
furniture, bedding, paint, and eco products
(415) 331-4364

acknowledgments

Mama: You are my hero...the real Wonder Woman. Thank you for allowing me to be a free spirit.

Granny and Papa: I will always be your Sugar. I hope I make you proud.

My Muny: What a gentle soul you are. I guess decorating really is in our blood.

My big brother Mark: Thanks for letting me always follow you around. You are a great leader. It really prepared me for my boys—stinky feet and all!

My little sister Jill, "Jilly Bean": I could not have chosen a better sister. You are my true best friend. We have been through a lot together. I am so proud of you. What an honor to watch you be a mommy. Thank you for all your help with this book. You are the other half of my brain. I really appreciate all of the laughs. I love you!

My sweet Elle, Auntie Elle to my boys: From the moment we met, I knew you were the only one for this project. What a wonderful journey we have had. Thank you for always believing in me and guiding this rookie to the finish line. How amazing that you could take these scattered thoughts and turn them into beautiful ones. We did it! Keep your eye out for hummingbirds.

My *Extreme Makeover: Home Edition* family: You know who you are. My, have we grown! Thank you for always accepting me with open arms.

Laurie Frankel: You are the true definition of a rock star. I never pictured this book without you. Thank you for bringing photographs to these words. I cannot think of another person I would rather take a red-eye with—drinking champagne and sharing life stories.

Nancy Hadley, "Nancy Pants": No words can describe the talent you possess. Thank you for all the fairy dust. You are a wonderful role model—we really can have it all!

Liz Brunwin: Muchas gracias for all your help getting us started.

Joseph Wahl: You have such a great sense of style. Thank you for all your contributions and hard work.

The Messner girls: Thank you for always making me a part of your family. Daddy Mez, thank you for stepping in. You are so missed. I will always be your Agent 47.

The mommies and daddies who had faith in me to take over their precious ones' nurseries: Thank you for giving me the space to create a beautiful book.

The wonderful companies that contributed so generously to this book: Thank you from the bottom of my heart. I really could not have done this without you.

Dan Ambrosio, my agent: I am so appreciative of your loyalty to me and to this book. Look how far we have come! Thanks enormously to you and David Vigliano.

Dervla Kelly, my editor: Thanks to you and Leslie Stoker for helping make my dream come true. It is nice to know that there are others on a "green mission."

Alissa Faden, my book designer: Wow, did I get lucky! You truly get my style. Thank you for bringing your extraordinary talent to every page.

Deb Young, mother of Evan and Eden: Many thanks for making sure the challenge of twins and the fine art of maximizing space were included in this book.

Jennifer Thompson, mom to Mick and Maddie: Your ideas for the perfect nursery came fast and furious—thanks so much. And don't worry, Jen – I know you're the true originator of monster spray.

Jan Fishler: Thanks for your endless supply of information on brain stimulation. Sasha and Nick are so fortunate to have you for a mom.

Cassandra Clark: Your early proofreading and skilled eye for typos prevented considerable embarrassment. Thanks enormously for the Jackson Pollock thing.

about the author

Tracy Hutson has been a stylist and designer since 1999, when she started her Los Angeles-based design business. With an eye on each client's individual lifestyle and unique taste, she has worked on remodeling projects that range from single rooms to entire homes.

In 2003, she became part of the design team on *Extreme Makeover: Home Edition*, and has witnessed firsthand the dramatic impact that living spaces have on the lives of the people who occupy them. Much of her design work on the show has focused on children's spaces, and as the mother of two little boys, nurseries are her current passion and priority. Tracy lives in the Los Angeles area with her family.